# Memoirs of A Religious Breakdown

*Written by*

## Sabrina Jones

www.rdtalleybooks.com

Plainsboro, New Jersey

Cover Designed by Alicia Pierce

ISBN: 978-1-7342540-6-8

R.D. Talley Books Publishing
P.O. Box 45
Plainsboro, New Jersey 08536
www.rdtalleybooks.com

## Dedication

To my mother Bettye:

"Sabrina, wipe your tears and cry later.

There is work to be done."

# Preface

Answered prayer can be a painful process. I know that now. As I reread some of the passages that I wrote eleven years ago, I can remember feeling like I was in a twilight zone while everyone else in my church and religious circles seemed to have this Jesus life down packed. I am now grateful for true freedom. It has not been easy. This was a lonely road in the beginning. I even had religious symptoms of withdrawals and my only antidote was the guidance of the Holy Spirit. There was safety in the rituals and being up under the religious "coverings". I was doing fine, until I decided that there had to be more.

My journey began back in 2009. There were a few tremors at first, but I thought it was just me needing to do "more", so to speak. I dismissed what I saw and heard. But the tremors soon turned into eruptions which constantly drove me to more deliverance, purging and praying. I was fine, until the next question arose within or the next "oddity" of a guest speaker. I questioned myself, doubted myself and truly found myself within a constant state of feeling that God was not pleased with me. I insulted my Father by begging for the grace and mercy that was so graciously granted, day by day, hour by hour and yes, sometimes, even minute by minute as I embarked on a long journey of being traumatized by this religious spirit. The sweetest voice in my ear was telling me that I was damned to hell for not "doing" enough for HIM. That sweet deceptive voice, just like the one that was in the Garden of Eden, was always telling me that I needed to do more to acquire favor with my Father as well as my religious superiors. For years, I idolized my leaders and idealized my religion. It was not until I got out of the dark that I was able to see the SON arise, that I was able to see the light! I asked HIM to lead me unto all truth and to open my eyes so that I could see. And when HE did, I argued within and to be honest, argued with HIM. How can this be wrong when it feels right and it looks right and I have been taught that it was right and was given this word and that word. So many times I thought that my healing came from what ran down my cheeks. But, in essence, my healing came when I began to hear HIM; a sweet voice filled with power and a love that was ready to lead me out of the religious bondage, by which I myself opened the doors and welcomed in. Throughout the awakening and healing process, I dared to share my experiences with a few brothers and sisters in Christ and I was amazed to find out that there is a remnant of who can truly relate. Many are trapped within this religious indoctrination and bondage whereas it has their identity connected to an umbilical cord. The cord holds the title, wealth, time, and their future. I am part of this remnant. And this is my story.

# Introduction

This is a diary of my thoughts and observations, as one who truly believes that she had a religious breakdown, if there is such a thing. I call it a religious breakdown because it was a spirit of religion, several traditions and twisted doctrines that had me almost to the point of feeling as if I was losing my mind. Many things that I had been told, taught or to believe in as a follower of Jesus Christ, I was now beginning to question within my heart. This was the first tremor, so to speak. Everyone knows that we are to never question or challenge a religious protocol. We are to follow the instructions and wait for the miracle to appear. The religious stance required me to do and perform certain actions in order to experience the benefits of HIS presence and it was at this point where I seemed to fail miserably, which I incubated this into a mindset of me failing as a Christian. For a season, I felt as if this spirit of religion was breaking me down. A constant state of repentance, always thinking that the Father was not pleased with me and living in fear of grieving the Holy Spirit. The formula did not work for me: $P = F+R+D/C$. The presence of God equals Fasting, plus, Reading the Word, plus

Devotionals divided by Church attendance. Really, I was in a state. Eventually, through the process of finding out exactly who I was in Christ, I began to fight back and eventually overcoming the grip that this religious spirit had on my soul, mind and body. Through this torment, I found myself questioning my salvation, God, Jesus, and the Holy Spirit. And oddly enough, when I prayed and asked for revelation and clarity on how I was feeling, when the answers came, I could not accept it! I must have a dendrite or neuron mixed up in my brain because most surely, I was missing something. So, I figured the only way to find my way out of this thicket was to start at ground zero, right at the point where I felt that I had crashed: Church.

But first, let me say that this little book is not all about a specific church or a denomination. Throughout my life, I have been indoctrinated within three major denominations and each one left a fingerprint to my breakdown, which I alone allowed and invited. But in all truth, this book is about me. My perceptions, whether true or false. These perceptions were cornerstones that I put in place. It is about those nouns and verbs that I allowed, as well as perceived to be truths that stressed me to a point where I began questioning my salvation. At times I ramble and at times, my words may not even seem to make sense; and that is because I could not make any sense of what I was going through during the time. Writing these memoirs through the years has been a tremendous help in allowing me to see myself and direct me where to place the blame (which is myself) and the balm. I am sure that I represent quite a few out there. I know that there will be some to whom it may appear that I have possibly read their diary, or mind for that matter; for I know all too well that what I have experienced has happened to many saints and is still prevalent in many of the institutionalized churches today. If you just happen to not be in that inner court of the elite prestigious, Nicolaitan class you will probably understand my thoughts, observations and sometimes just plain rants. If you are part of that elite class previously mentioned, then you may not comprehend my pain and may simply consider me to be "out of order" or rebellious. I am fully aware that for some, the institutional religious church and all that it encompasses is their life and they are completely happy. For some, it holds the seams to their status and livelihood. Good for you. But for me, I was not satisfied. Something was wrong… and for years I thought it was ALL me. This little book is not about church bashing. If you are not part of the institutionalized religious church system and you are centered on HIS Kingdom, then you have no need to be offended or quick to shoot your arrow. You should agree with many things that I will share. God knows those whose livelihood and status depend upon this system have their own armory of comebacks and protective grenades to throw the moment one criticizes their building or how they keep their flock. But we tend to protect what feeds us and keeps us nourished. I on the other hand, was malnourished and I felt as if I were dying. Dying both ways, in this world of ours and in this world of hours.

## Something Is Not Right, and It Must Be Me...

I believe I may need some deliverance. There is no way I can be saved feeling the way I feel. I think I need somebody to slap me. Yeah, slap me so hard that my flesh will run and hide so that my spirit man will take the reins, because this is not how it is supposed to be. Y'all, we had a guest speaker tonight at church and I declare he said something that sounded completely off, to the point that I wanted to just walk out. My face, my face, my face said it all and I quickly had to fix it. Yet, when I looked around to see if anybody heard what I heard or to see if anyone else had a "raised brow", it was as if the entire room was fogged up and I was standing alone in a spotlight. It felt as if everyone was in on the secret but me. As he kept talking, the crowd went wild. There was the usual shouting and hollering along with a few saints running up to the altar and throwing money on it, which of course made our guest speaker "perform" all the more. I mean, it was as if a huge joy bubble had burst and everyone caught the spirit but me. I wanted to get in on this joy. I wanted to feel what everyone around me was feeling. I was ready to give in. Even if he was saying "off" things. I wanted to shout until I got my breakthrough like every other hopping, popping, and stomping saint. After "reaching for my blessing, spinning around three times, high fiving and turning to my neighbor for the thirtieth time", I just stopped trying to "get it". I could not even fake it like in previous times before. I found myself sitting down while the crowd went wild feeling as if I had not been let in on the script or secret.

This seems to be happening a lot. I wonder, what is wrong with me? I really wished that I had just stayed home, but my Pastor said for everyone to be back on tonight and I wanted to be obedient to my leader. I have prayed that the Lord would give me some type of insight, wisdom or understanding as to what I am going through. But to be honest, the more I inquire about it, the more I feel confused. My mind is always churning. Lord, how I wish that I could turn it off! Maybe I am not really saved…Or maybe there is a deep generational curse in action…or maybe I am mentally ill. How can I be thinking such negative things about the man of God and still be saved? Afterall, this speaker (who is as predictable as the sunset) was still a man of God. All night he has said nothing but the usual church clichés and asked everyone to turn to their neighbor at least 30 times! Sigh...I am embarrassed to even write this, but I do not like going to church sometimes. I am cringing now because next week is an annual conference. Sigh again...I don't want to go even though it is mandatory. I don't want to hear the same old phrases, I don't want to turn to my neighbor, I don't want to repeat after me and say...I don't want to high five three people and say...I don't want to listen to all the formalities related to someone's own personal agendas, I don't want to wear white and I don't want to turn to the person behind me either. As I have re-read what I have written, I see that it sounds completely out of order. Rebellious, I am sure some would say.

Maybe I need to fast and spend some time alone with God...because something is not right. I wonder if I am depressed and just don't know it. If I got a demon, I want it out. I want to be saved...

## The Torment of Regret

She would often beg me to come home to visit and even
though I was only a few hours away, I always made excuses.
Those times when I did come, I always had to hurry back.
"All you do is go to church", she often said. She was right. I
had made church my idol, and for years, nothing and no one
came before it. And now she is gone. Grief is one thing, but
when it is riddled with guilt and regret, it begins to damn
your very soul. I cry until I am dry, and I find myself
recalling every conversation and argument about me coming
to visit. I am angry, I am hurt, and I am ashamed. How could
I have done this to the greatest mother of all? This is eating
me inside and out. I put on a good front, but inside I am
jacked up. How did I get to this point? It looks like I have
built a great garrison to a mindset that I myself have created.
I need help. The torment of regret can keep you from moving
forward.

## Feeling Like A Lost Sheep

I saw a post where one of the Pastors were talking about *his* sheep. They said, "My sheep know when to come home…it is so good to have sheep that are loyal to their leaders…"

Years of passing through hallways during large meetings, I have heard sayings such as these and many other things. I remember taking on the concept of acting and behaving as "dumb". I thought that dumbing down myself and hanging my head down was how to be. The security and evidence of my salvation and growth was centered around me exemplifying total submission to my shepherd. Therefore, whatever he asked me to do, I did it. It could have been anything. I am sorry to admit it, but at one point I was so caught up that had he asked me to eat grass, I would have. Like many, I felt that I could not think for myself. Submission, obedience, availability, accountability, subjection to authority was how I pleased God. If I honored my Pastor, then I honored God. I was loyal to the leader to the point where at times, I forsook all, even my family, to accommodate his request. Failing even to visit my mother, who often begged me to come visit her just a few hours away. When it came to church, nothing else mattered. Isn't Jesus our Shepherd? I feel so lost right now. Loyalty is a virtue. But I now see how I have allowed myself to take it to the extreme. This little lamb feels lost right now and I need the Good Shepherd to help me get back on track. I have some resentment. I have guilt and shame. I love my shepherd, but I just don't feel like following him right now. I don't agree with his request. Oh-M-Gee…I feel bad about how I feel.

## Afterthought

The Bible says that His sheep know His voice. Well, I hear you. I am in pain and I hear You calling me. I hear Your voice of reason and Your voice of compassion.
Pain…amazing how it can cause a silence within allowing you to hear.

## Rantings In My Head...

I am trying not to cry as I write this, but the tears are falling. I am tired! I am tired of you! I am tired of your tiered hierarchies. Like the Nicolaitans, you like to separate everyone according to rank.

*The name "Nicolaitans" comes from the Greek word Nikolaos, which is combination of two Greek words; Nikos and Laos. Nikos means to conquer or subdue. Laos means the people. It is also where we get that dreaded word often thrown out to the pews, laity. Together, they form Nicolas, which literally means one who conquers and subdues the people.*

You have those elites who sit in decorated seats elevated high with outstretched hands. Can you not see that it is Jezebel who is handing you that golden goblet to which you desire to sip out of? I'm also tired of your titles: The Right Reverend, the Archbishop Elite, the Great Elite Apostle, Cardinal Supreme, the Reverend Doctors, and the Honored Queens. What's next? Ayatollah, Your Diocese? Jezebel's breath can bend the hairs on your eyelashes, yet you cannot even see her. I am also tired of meeting your deadlines, by which I often met at any cost to myself and family only for my calls and pleas to go unanswered or better yet, ignored. Oh yes, I have seen first-hand how you screen calls. I guess that is normal. When you needed me, I was there and now when I need you, all I hear are crickets. I am tired of the loud organs and booming drums accompanied with rhythmic clichés. I am tired of you and your protocols and religious customs. Does every Elder have to moan during his sermon? Elder? Do you have to preach to the tempo of an organ? Do you? That screaming…I see you, the hock back oyster gagging, hooping, hollering, and spit wiping hanky, "Turn to ya neighbor"; high five three people; repeat after me; touch the person behind you; turn around three times; SENSATIONALISTIC PIMP! And once more I feel alone. I feel like I have been dredged in gasoline and I am on my way to hell. Hundreds ran to the offering line. Truly, religion has its own language and dialect and it demands feedback.

## Religious Schizophrenia

I am also tired of twisted doctrines. The pants that you don't want me to wear are split down the middle. One leg says that I can wear those pants and the other leg says I cannot and that I am sinning. Same with this head covering thing. Some say that my head must be covered, while others say that I can go without it. You train me to go tell the world about Him and then you tell me I can't go. I need to serve at "home". You tell me to give *this* seed to get *that* blessing, and then ask me to give a special offering just to seal the blessing. I am a worthless sinner, saved by grace. True. And yet I am the righteousness of God and the old man has been put away. Some say, "Let Jesus come into your heart", while others scream, "No, repent before God and believe". They said that if I left the building, I would be cursed and something bad would happen to me. Yet, to remain has me feeling like I am cursed. You said that I had no opinion and no voice, yet at your command you want me to encourage you and give you shouts of amen. You said I must have a spiritual covering, yet in no way have I seen your support or encouragement. Coverings... hmm... Is that even biblical?

As my eyes begin to open, I see the ugliness of it all and yet, I feel trapped because I do not know what to do. I created this. I allowed it to happen. I held my Pastor's words equal to the Word of God and the Bible was a supplement. Had I read the Bible on my own... had I studied on my own... had I asked the Holy Ghost to lead me and guide me unto all truth on my own, I would not be in the place I am in. I feel like a coward, but I cannot play this church game anymore, nor can I blame anyone. To be honest, I have no one to blame but myself. I wanted to be accepted by my leadership. I wanted my leader to be proud of me, and to be honest, at times I wanted to sit on the front row. I wanted my name called and I wanted to be recognized. To me, he was like Papa and I wanted attention from Papa. Wrong Papa. LOL...interesting how I would run from the spotlight now. I want no parts of it at all! Thank God for this journal where I can express how jacked-up I feel. We have to be careful not to make idols out of our leaders. It is dangerous for us and it is dangerous for them. These days, people come to Christ and the church immediately begin their indoctrination processes. Their rules and expectations. "We believe this. We do that. We don't do that. We don't believe in that. We have this event every Tuesday. This offering is expected every Friday night. This is mandatory. Those seats belong to leadership." You get the picture. Somewhere along the way, the relationship with Christ gets intertwined with the religious church system.

Do I sound angry? I am, but more so confused. I need to stop right here and pray, ask the Lord to help me get on the right path again. I feel so lost...but one thing for sure. I WANT TO BE SAVED.

## More and More

The weight of "more" is more crushing than the remedy of "more". I fail so eloquently at more. More prayer, more fasting, more reading, more church, more study, more sacrifice, more giving and more conference attendance. More makes me feel like a failure and a disappointment to God. I raise the bar and every time I try to do more, I fall short. I thought that the remedy of "more" would help me to become more spiritual and get closer to God. It cannot be this complicated. I know there has to be more, but must I do more?

## Fighting Crazy

The fight is on. I woke up almost in a ritualistic mode with a bunch of fleeces to throw. Immediately, I began to plan MY agenda. "Okay, I am going to pray... then read some Word... then pray again, watch my confessions and..." and then I felt something within me saying, "Hold up!" I then decided not to do any of that. My focus shifted to one thing and that was making certain of my salvation and understanding my salvation. I went deep within. Deep into my character and I asked myself a question: "Do you really desire to have a relationship with the Father?" My honest response was this: *Yes, but I am not ready. I got some things I need to work on in me to become more spiritual...I need to get more in my word and prayer more.*

Wow...I am shocked at my own truthful response! So, in order for me to have relationship with God, I need to do more Godly things. This mindset is a problem! God, help me! I feel like I am losing it...but at least I am not willing to punk out. I could visually see my mind throwing out file after file of religious doctrines and habits. To be honest, I had a hard time letting go of some of these strongholds, but I had to keep going back to my own ground zero and build back up. The first step of rebuilding was to make sure that my foundation was solid. I sought the Holy Spirit and my prayer was very simple, but sincere: "Lead and guide me to the Truth". The breakdown begins...

## In The Matrix

I was watching *The Matrix* a few nights ago and something really jumped out at me...Like Neo, I feel like I am living in a Matrix. Something is just not right. How can saints of the Most-High God applaud and defend those things that our FATHER clearly labels as sin? A friend of mine was telling me the other day about a Pastor who said that he could not bring himself to forgive another individual. To me, it is as simple as ABC and 123. As a disciple of Christ, you must forgive. Yet, we have such great pettiness within the body. The hater messages are at an all-time high and coaching has become the new form of pastoring. The other night I was crying out to the Father asking HIM to help me because I am always feeling that I am missing the boat. Everyone seems to have a "shout" for the clichéd messages, but me. Everyone seems excited as they run to sow into the "Seal Your Blessing" offering, but me. It seems like everyone knows the vision of the leader and they are all drenched in humility and submission, but me. "What is wrong with meeeeee?!?!?" I keep asking and begging the Father to reveal this demon or curse, because I do not want to miss God. I do not want to be left behind. This has been going on for about two years. I keep going back and forth and it seems that as the Lord begins to open my eyes, here comes another battle.

## Distractions From Within

Keeping my mind on HIM today…Well, trying to. I can
begin to pray and think on those things that are holy and the
next thing I know, I am thinking of what I want for dinner,
how dirty my window blinds are, thinking about weird
security questions; things like *what was the address of my
Elementary school?*, to seeing if I can name all of my
elementary grade school teachers. When I do a mental audit
trail, I am amazed at how I come to these thoughts. Indeed,
the mind can be a loose cannon ready to fire off in any
direction. At least my mind can. My thoughts can be about
how Jesus healed the sick and actually seeing myself praying
for someone who needs healing, to instantly finding myself
thinking about someone else I know who needs prayer due to
a stroke…A name pops in my head. *I remember now, and her
name is "CC"*, the next thing I know I am thinking about
someone else named "CC" from New Jersey! My mind
wanders to *"CC" and now* I begin to wonder where she is
now. I am remembering details! And here goes the tangent
trail: *I can see her face now, we used to walk to Elementary
school together. She had a cute brother, he had purple coach*

*converse sneakers…my mom always brought me cheap sneakers… that walk seemed so long, but it was only to… man, what street was that? Oh yeah, North 7th Street. What was that address there I used to know it…* Wow, see how I get off track! So, today I am catching myself as I wander and really trying to focus on HIM. Making everything about HIM makes me stay more focused on HIM. What I am not doing is making it hard. It takes a desire and a will to stay focused on HIM. I cannot think for a moment that the enemy gets sad when I get distracted. Distractions are toxic. He gave me this beautiful creative mind. I need to renew it.

## In This Order: Jesus, Kingdom, Family, Work, Church

Through the years, I have often heard these phrases:

"If you can go to work, then you can go to church (ecclesia)."

"If you can be on time for work, then you can be on time for church."

"If you can go to work after being up late, you can come to church."

I am sure you get the picture. Well, I was thinking about that and what I am going to say will get a lot of side-eyed reading, but to tell you the truth and what most lay members think when this comes across a pulpit. My job comes before church and please let me explain why. You see for now I have to work a job. I would prefer to have my own business, but for now I must work to keep shelter, healthcare, and maintain a pantry of food as well as keep transportation. My job provides income to allow me to live a healthy and productive lifestyle. My job also supplies the green paper to keep the lights on in the church. I get to work on time, because if I fail to do so it could possibly cause me to lose this job, which would in turn stop my supply of funding and thus my contribution to church. I work so that I can be a blessing to the church as well as others. I love giving. I also go to work every day because…well, I have to. If I did not have to work, I probably would not, although I do like my job. I receive not just regular benefits, but promotions and gifts have come due to my commitment, work ethic and services. I like where I work, but who wouldn't want to run their own ship? So yes church, my job comes ahead of you. If I had to choose between getting fired and coming to church, I'd choose my job. I'd really have to though. You see church, you are not in a position to help me. Let hard times come and let's see who calls to ask you if you need help paying your light bill. The fact is, I have witnessed people behind on their rent and the ecclesia did very little to assist them. Church folks lose houses, cars and property just like the world does and the ecclesia just can't help them. The church has a $7,000 bank note to pay, plus a $2,000 electric bill. And oh, if you needed $16K for a lifesaving surgery, you may need to get your house in order because the best that the ecclesia can do for you is put you on the prayer list. So, the next time this condemning comment comes across a pulpit, I am just going to smile and look ahead knowing that HE comes first, then my family, job and lastly, church.

## Widows

You can really tell a lot about a ministry by how they treat their widows. ALL OF THEM. Uhh…yeah. I am going to pay more attention and try to help those whom the Bible has directed us to care for.

## Shaking Inside and Shaking My Head

I disagreed with a leader and voiced my opinion too loudly.
You would think that I committed the unpardonable sin with
the stares I got. I believe a few even backed away from what
I could see from my peripheral vision. I am so tired, and I am
so confused. Now, I am a rebellious woman who needs to be
corrected. You should have heard the rebukes in love that
came pouring out. I am ashamed to write what I feel like
doing to myself. But really, I am getting to the point where I
feel like I am losing it again. I have no opinion, no voice, and
no input. Sounds like a slave, don't it?

## I Have To Do Better

I left out of a leadership meeting with swells of tears in my eyes, which I dared not to let one drop. I refused to blink as I sat there concentrating on not allowing my beloved leader to see a tear fall. Walking out, I felt limp and bruised; as if I had been in a boxing match. "Maybe I should not take this too seriously," I thought to myself. "No one else seems to be bothered." I heard the battle horns in my head as another mental battle began. "How can I not take my salvation seriously?"

The meeting was a call for us to do better, to be more consecrated and committed to the vision of the house. Our services were needed. Volunteers were needed. Our finances were needed. Our time was needed. All for the glory of God. My beloved leader explained the expanded vision and reminded us of our mission statement. It all sounded good, but I was beginning to feel overwhelmed. I know he was not talking to me personally about being "sold out", but I took it that way. I was wondering what else I could do to be more "sold out". I am already at church three to four days a week.

All day on Sundays, midweek service, Tuesday night classes and sometimes more. I have all too often rushed home from work, threw meals together, garnished the kids, sniffed my arms, spread gel on my fly a ways, dressed in a flash and zoomed to church. How I would have loved to come walking in looking calm, flawless, and fresh.

I took the classes, paid for the workshops, traveled at times and did my best to sow into the special offerings. And yet, my beloved leader stands before us basically demanding more. I felt like a failure and I got angry with myself. I called myself lazy and unorganized. It was my fault that I was not as spiritual as my leader needed me to be. So, as my beloved leader's vision grew, so did my routine of religious activities. Ask me how that worked for me...uh, yeah.

## The 5:30 Prayer Fiasco

Well, here I am doing more…I started going to 5:30 am prayer. I had hoped that this would help me in my pursuit of getting closer to God and building a relationship with Jesus. But instead, it did not. Tell me, how can you go to a 5:30 am prayer and come back feeling defeated and manifesting in a state worse than before?!!!! Only I could do that. Am I a heretic? My mind begins to wander. *Am I a descendent from Cain or the Amalekites or worse?* When I arrived, the music was playing softly and I heard a few muffled prayers, but within ten minutes of praying I would find myself dozing off. I felt so bad about it. I mean I could have just stayed at home in bed and prayed for ten minutes ya know. The next issue arrived when someone started screaming out their prayers and petitions very loudly. I mean really loud. Really like off the decibel chain! I could not focus or concentrate, due to her screams which had loud screeching wails of "Jeeeezzzzus" every few seconds. Here I am in a prayer meeting and saying within myself, "I wish she would just shut up, so we can all pray!" And when I saw that the Elder in charge was not going to address her, I got bothered all the more and moved far away to another section to really try to "deal with my flesh", repent about wanting to stuff a baseball in my sisters mouth and talk to the Father. But then, I get disturbed again because now the Elder in charge is asking all of us to gather up to the front. We are then given hand-outs on what to pray. Word for word. We are instructed to pray in unison for the church, the first family of the church, the nations, marriages, children, the city, etc. We do that, dismiss and go home. As I drove back home to get ready for work, I kept asking myself what was the purpose of this? After I cried and beat myself up for feeling the way I did, I continued going to the morning prayer even though I did not like it, until eventually I just stopped. What did I expect? I expected for it to be a place where we could share what we were feeling and ask for prayer, as well as pray for one another over "their" issues. I expected intimacy. I thought we would pray for the sick and pray as led by the Holy Ghost. Yeah...I really thought that the fire of God would meet us all there at 5:30 am because after all, we arose early to meet HIM. I am ashamed of how I feel...Lord, I want to be saved.

# I Just Decided To Shut Up and Keep Walking

The protocols of religion are exhausting and will have you
feeling like you are a substandard being. Religion has always
reminded me that I have a proper code to follow and that I
must behave a special way toward my leaders. In most
instances, I just remained silent so that I would not say
anything stupid or out of order accidentally. I often listened to
others who were advised that in the company of your leader
amongst other leaders, one was not allowed to speak.
Actually, proper religious etiquette says for me to remove
myself from their presence and only speak when spoken to.
Even to laugh or smile too hard could be considered out of
order. Did you know that you are supposed to walk behind
your superiors? Did you know that you should never talk to
them while standing if they are seated? Did you know that
you are to bend down on your knee to communicate and you
should never use the arm of their chair to raise yourself up?
This stuff is actually taught! No wonder why so many like
myself are jacked-up and see our beloved leaders as
unapproachable. To be honest, I always felt a sense of fear
whenever I was around them. Scared I was going to say

something stupid. I mean if I am not good enough to complement your shoes or say good morning, then how am I good enough to even be in your presence? Religious titles demand respect and honor from the laity and some leaders do expect to be treated in a certain way. It is what this system has bred. Seats are reserved with a dainty little hanky draped on the back with bottles of *Perrier* nearby on cute little serving tables, while I've seen a single mother with babies struggling to find a seat. *Sigh and cry.*

I never was able to fit in. Even when I wanted to! I always looked awkward, or out of place. Some people have their comfort zone in all of these religious protocols. For me, the opposite is true and always has been. I just played along to fit in.

I passed an Elder in the hall earlier this evening and I spoke. He looked right through me and kept walking. Next time, I guess I will just shut up and keep walking too.

## I Feel So Lost

I have been praying that the Lord would direct me to the right path, because I feel as if the path that I am on is the business church interstate, so to speak. I sense that something is not right with our western church as a whole. Am I the only one who sees this?! There has to be more, but I feel as if I am the only one seeing/feeling this, but I know that I cannot be the only one. I wish that I could get on the bypass and focus on the destination instead of having to deal with so much religious fluff. Just thinking…I know that these people are saved and that their intent may be good…but deep down within my soul, I just know that something is not right. If I am the problem, then please, please, please FATHER send a detour right away and get me on the right path. If it is indeed this system of religion that has me feeling so heavy, then help me to gain the strength to break free of this grasp. I want you intensely Jesus, My King! But what do I do when the very system that got me trapped is the only way I know to get to you? Attend all services, serve, pray for an hour…fast for three days, put on worship music…read a certain amount of Bible chapters each day, pray in the spirit for one hour, honor my leadership, obey...submit... pay my tithes...sow, sow, and sow some more. The system just sucks you dry. There has to be more to serving you than this. There has to be more.

## Am I Saved? Why Am I Feeling Like This?

I feel so detached right now. Why is it that I feel that by not
going to a church service, it makes me feel like I am not
saved?!! I feel that I am doing something wrong if I miss a
service. I feel as if I have backslidden. How do you explain
the fact that I want to be in His presence, yet I do not want to
go to church? Father, please help me! I do not want to put on
a dress, stockings, hot curl my hair and lightly beat my face. I
just don't feel like it. I feel this weight upon me. Like I am
letting people down and sinning by not going to church, and
then I make excuses bordering a lie trying to defend why I
wasn't there to others. I feel that if I don't go then God will
not be pleased with me. I am feeling so torn right now…I
write this with tears swelling in my eyes…On one hand, I
don't want to go and on the other hand, I feel obligated to
go. I missed communion too. To be honest I feel terrible and
so unworthy. I am praying to you, O' Father, as I write this. I
desire to know you in spirit and in truth. I do not want to be
deceived or fake. Please Holy Spirit…lead me and guide me
to all truth. Please help me. Give me the comfort, peace, and
joy that only you can give me. I hate religion; but yet I am

craving it! This is bondage! Even now, I am fighting the very essence of what is keeping me from my freedom. I am fighting to keep from performing some religious ritual so that the Father will not be angry with me for not going to church.

*"What is more, I consider everything a loss because of the surpassing worth of knowing Christ Jesus my Lord, for whose sake I have lost all things. I consider them garbage, that I may gain Christ and be found in him, not having a righteousness of my own that comes from the law, but that which is through faith in Christ—the righteousness that comes from God on the basis of faith."*
*Philippians 3:8-9, NIV*

## Afterthought

Some of my friends who are reading this will think of me as being carnal by saying this. It is okay, because I say this out of a carnal emotion. But, if I could go to church braless...I sho' nuff would do it. I hate wearing them and getting all girdled-up and lifted is one of the main reasons why I jet out of there after service. I be ready to get home and sling all that stuff off and get free!

## Another Thought

I am church and church is me. If I decide not to go then guess what? I am not going to hell. Tired of how these elite bullies throw shade on members who do not appear visible within the ministry. They're working. They're tired. They're cleaning their house! They ain't got a maid like you do.

Quotes that made me cringe...

*"I love obedient sheep who honor their pastor"*

*"Our sheep know their leader's voice and heart"*

*"When you honor your leader, you honor the Lord"*

*"Saints don't want to serve anymore. They're missing their blessing"*

## Stuck

Joshua 10:13 (NIV) "So the sun stood still, and the moon stopped…"

Lord, please direct me to the right path. I do not like the critical church bashing person that I have become. I sense that something is not right. I believe that there is more and yes, I know these people are saved and that their intent may be good…but deep down within my soul, I just know something is wrong. If it is wrong with me, then please, please, please send a detour right away and get me on the right path. If it is indeed this system of religion, then help me to gain the strength to break free of this grasp. I want You extremely bad and the very system that I feel trapped in is the only way I know to get to You. Pray for an hour… Put on worship music… Read my Bible for one hour… . Obey… Submit… Pay my Tithes… Lord, I do love You and Your people…. Please help me. I feel stuck, like I am just hanging.

## Serving

I volunteered to work with hospitality last night. To be
honest, I volunteered because I do not like conferences where
I have to sit and listen to a dozen or more acknowledgements,
watch a few peculiar acting men shout, listen to offering
sermons and hear a lot of whooping and hollering. So, this
was a way to be there but not be there. Anyway, I love
serving and entertaining, plus the cooks in my church are off-
the-chain as well as clean. Did you hear me say
"clean"? Therefore, I volunteered and was given the beginner
job of "beverage maiden", which was the simple task of
keeping everyone's drink filled. Now, this special dinner that
I was serving at was not for everyone. It was for the Elders,
Pastors, Bishops, denominational bigwigs, visiting guests, etc.
who came to the conference and were invited to a **private
dinner** after service. The rest of the church had to wait in line
down the hall for their fried fish or head tail to McDonald's.

The décor was beautiful, especially the head table. I was not
allowed to go near the head table, only seasoned hospitality
members who knew what they were doing were allowed to

service these special guests. They would be seated at a head table, usually with a beautifully displayed centerpiece. Anyway, once the benediction was said, those hungry elites poured in along with their adjutants. A few were very friendly and even greeted me, while others looked right pass me or directly at me and for reasons that they only know, refused to speak. No problem though. I was not there to socialize or make friends. My purpose was to serve coffee, tea, and water. Now, it was my intent to act like a pro at this, after all I had waited tables to pay for college. But I must admit, I probably looked like a novice by staring with my mouth opened when I saw an adjutant pull out bedroom slippers and place them on a First Lady's feet. I did not care too much for a couple of the visiting adjutants. They made it clear that they "outranked" us. Yeah…I had to quickly check myself. After all, I had to respect the fact that for some, this was their ministry and they truly loved serving in this capacity. I have now come to realize that this type of serving is not for me. As a matter of fact, I had already decided after this conference was over, it would be my last time serving in this capacity. I respect those who do…but it is not for me!

Anyway, by now the aroma of the rosemary herbed chicken had my tummy growling and I found myself uttering a selfish prayer that there would be enough food left over for those of us serving to eat. So, you can imagine my delight when I learned about the leftover rule. Everyone who served was allowed to eat after everyone was gone and we could carry extra food home to boot! What benefits one gets for serving! If we did eat early, of course we had to eat out of site. You cannot have the help eating with or in front of the leaders. Initially, I failed miserably at being a beverage maiden. No one told me to pour the pitcher from the side, so unfortunately a couple of Elders got baptized with tea. Luckily for me, I knew them very well and they were very understanding and did not make too much of a fuss. We even shared a laugh about it. However, the hospitality leader was not happy! She was known for having a reputation of perfection when it came to events like this. So, I got the stare of disbelief. After another hour or so, I believe I had achieved redemption by way of pouring correctly and keeping everyone's water, tea, and coffee current. After a while, I was finally able to rest by standing up against the wall in my black dress with my hands folded neatly in front. As a hospitality "maiden", you are to stand far back enough so that you cannot hear the conversations being said, but close enough so that you can quickly address needs as summoned. Just like any hotel plated dinner or fine dining restaurant, except you are not getting paid. Hmm…I wonder has anyone ever gotten a holy handshake by way of serving this way. I think tips should be allowed; I am just saying. Now as the hour hit 1:00 am, I could feel my tiredness coming on. Most of the men cleared out, but it was a few of the elite ladies who remained. I don't care how many times you yawn or how often the light flicker. These ladies will talk all night if they could. Well, actually, they did. All I could think of was that I had to get up at six and be to work tomorrow, and then turn around and be back in position as beverage maiden again that evening. I guess when you can sleep until 9:00 or 10:00, staying up late is no problem. But this lady had to get up early and I was getting frustrated, so I walked up to the hospitality leader and told her that I was going to fix my plate and go. She was cool with that. Very understanding. I went in and made myself and my husband, who was probably snoring at home, a healthy plate and started on my way. I looked in on a few of the other servants. I saw a few of them still lined up against the wall, looking tired, hungry and sleepy. I blew them a kiss and walked to my car. Nope! After this event, no more for me. I'd rather watch two-year olds.

## Feeling Fake

I gathered toward the center of the sanctuary, as I was instructed to do. Knowing exactly why all of the ladies were asked to remain after service, I sat attentively and plastered a fake smile across my face. I am supposed to be excited about this...I am supposed to *want* to do this...after all, the Bible says to give honor to whom all honor is due, and the laborer is worthy of his hire. So, again I find myself in this familiar place of where my brain and heart begin to argue. I can hear the battle horns blowing in my mind, while the value of my spiritual worth begins plummeting to minus zero. "The tri-yearly love offering." Each woman is asked to give the First Lady a love offering, and of course a dollar amount is suggested. I absent-mindedly searched the crowd for her at first, forgetting that it would be considered not to be kosher for her to sit within the very crowd that is being asked to sow monetarily into her. That would be awkward. Our spokesperson proceeds to explain how awesome my First Lady is and how she is a friend to everyone; always there, always loving and caring for each and every one of us. She justifies why this blessing is so deserved, as well as several other positive adverbs to describe the noun. But one word popped out at me. The word "friend". I almost rebuked myself out loud for thinking what I did. "This lady has never been a friend to me", I thought to myself. I do not mean that in a hateful way. I like my First Lady. I love her as a sister in the Lord. Sure, she is pretty, always being nice and treats me kind whenever I have ventured away from my normal exit to say hello to her; but no, we are not friends. And besides, we probably could never be friends because it would be against the "code". I now begin to think of a quote from an Archbishop's wife, "Your First Lady is not your girlfriend. You cannot just pick up the phone and call her or address her just any kind of way. There has to be a line drawn for laity and leadership. They are not on your same level". Makes me think of Queen Elizabeth or Michelle Obama, although I would think I would have a better shot at becoming a real friend to one of them than even my own First Lady.

I sit here feeling like a phony, as I clap in agreement plastered with a cheesy grin on my face as I receive one of the specially printed rose-colored offering envelopes. I know that no one is putting a gun to my head, but I guess I am more concerned about why I am feeling this way. Again...am I missing the "love offering" gene? I already know that I do not have the "shopping gene" as most women do, so here I am thinking that something is wrong with me because I feel the way I feel. I look around at a few of her "handmaidens", who act as if they are investing in gold during a bull market. I can understand their excitement. They know her. They have waited on her, guarded her, assisted her and have done more for her than I probably will ever know, therefore I guess they have come to appreciate her and vice versa. But as for me, I don't know her. I only know that she is very sophisticated. She dresses very nice, she speaks well, sings well, is educated, she walks tall, and acts like a lady at all times. She sits in the same reserved spot every Sunday and will greet you with a warm hug if you approach her after service. I have nothing negative to say about her. As a matter of fact, I wish I had a burning desire to give to her. I once did, you know. I remember I made her a gift with my own two hands. Even had to order a few parts to assemble it. I believe that I really made it out of love at the time. I was excited about it. I admit, later on I yearned to hear if she liked it. I wanted to know if she had even worn it. As time went on, I assumed she gave it to a niece out of state or threw it in a seldomly used bottom drawer. I got one of those myself. It hurts my back when I bend down to open it. This was my own fault. I was ignorant enough to think that she would thank me. I guess I need to get rid of pride. I now feel that I should rebuke myself. Yet I still do not want to give in this offering. When I looked up *Love Offerings*, this is what it said… "made directly from a donor to a minister or church employee are generally not taxable to the recipient. These are considered personal gifts and are not deductible as a charitable contribution by the donor." I am such a terrible Christian to feel the way I feel. God please help me. As I read what I wrote…I feel worse.

*Later that day…*

<u>Why Am I Making This Hard?</u>

I believe that every believer should give whole heartedly to expand the Kingdom of God. I also believe that leaders should be fairly compensated for their work in the ministry. The Bible directs it. In 1 Corinthians 9, Paul clearly states that he's worth his wages: 1 Corinthians 9:7-11 (New American Standard Bible) *Who at any time serves as a soldier at his own expense? Who plants a vineyard and does not eat the fruit of it? Or who tends a flock and does not use the milk of the flock? I am not speaking these things according to human judgment, am I? Or does not the Law also say these things? For it is written in the Law of Moses, "YOU SHALL NOT MUZZLE THE OX WHILE HE IS THRESHING." God is not concerned about oxen, is He? Or is He speaking altogether for our sake? Yes, for our sake it was written, because the plowman ought to plow in hope, and the thresher to thresh in hope of sharing the crops. If we sowed spiritual things in you, is it too much if we reap material things from you?*

1 Corinthians 9:15-18 The Message (MSG)

*Still, I want it made clear that I've never gotten anything out of this for myself, and that I'm not writing now to get something. I'd rather die than give anyone ammunition to discredit me or impugn my motives. If I proclaim the Message, it's not to get something out of it for myself. I'm compelled to do it, and doomed if I don't! If this was my own idea of just another way to make a living, I'd expect some pay. But since it's not my idea but something solemnly entrusted to me, why would I expect to get paid? So am I getting anything out of it? Yes, as a matter of fact: the pleasure of proclaiming the Message at no cost to you. You don't even have to pay my expenses!*

If anybody was worthy of wages, it was Paul! But yet, he says it is just a mere pleasure proclaiming the gospel. You know, countless times I've heard leaders use Paul as a pattern for Christian living, but this scripture right here seems to get lost in the offering tray. I still do not want to give a love offering. Lord, is this wrong of me?

## I Need Deliverance

Romans 12:2 (KJV) "Be ye transformed by the renewing of your mind."

The Bible says to renew your mind. Well, I know for sure that the first thing that I need to do is get my mind out of my mind. Ephesians 4:22-24 (KJV) tells me to "...*put off* concerning the former conversation (behavior) the old man (old self), which is corrupt according to the deceitful lusts; and be *renewed in the spirit of your mind*; and that ye put on the new man (the new self), which after God is created in righteousness and true holiness." I am amazed at where my mind can take me at times. My sister surely got it right; it is a battlefield indeed. I mean, at times it is almost like a tug of war. Pulling down strongholds (mindsets) and taking thoughts captive! I got some POW's deep within my soul who, no matter how long they stay locked up, they yearn to escape and wreak havoc! I think it is time to kill these POW's.

Renewing this mind is a decision and a matter of the heart. I need to ask myself, "How do I see myself within my heart?", (the real me...the subconscious that is created by the conscious). Time to get free, kill the POW's and renew my thinking as well as my indulgences. Lord, I desire to be saved.

# When the Truth Hits You Like A Ton of Bricks, It Hurts.

I drove five hours south to basically a ghost town to get some deliverance. I was desperate and in pain. I failed at every single thing! Fasting, praying…nothing seemed to work. I truly felt as if I were having a religious breakdown. Constantly having crying fits over feeling as if I have disappointed my FATHER. Hating the things that I would think about what was happening during certain services, scared for my leadership to look me in the eye because they might see something. Just feeling worthless to the body. Repenting over and over again and wondering when the curse was going to come upon me for feeling like I did. Most of what I have been told concerning salvation, I have often found myself challenging it. Amazing how I can minster to everyone and they seem to get what they need, but when it comes to me, I hear crickets. I wonder, what did I do wrong? How come my Father seems like He is angry with me? I know He loves me, but I feel so empty and all alone.

Yet, I still believe and I am hoping that my one on one deliverance session will reveal something. I like the fact that it is one on one.

## Later On This Day...

Well...I was speechless when they said it and prior to today, had anyone ever said such to me I would have probably called them a bad word. @#$% liar. First, let me tell you that they did identify "worry" and "grief", and I felt the relief as these spirits departed. But when a nine-year old girl in deliverance training told me that she saw a religious spirit and that I was bound by my leadership, and under a spirit of Jezebel, I almost fainted. She even drew a picture of how she saw me in the spirit. A spear going through my head down through my body into the ground where I could not move. It was this sweet little adorable blonde-headed child that saw it and revealed it to me. Not only that, these people took notes and then compared them. There was confirmation upon confirmation of what the little darling saw! I wept right there, to the point where someone came over and placed their hands over my heart and prayed for my heart to be healed! The burst came forth because I knew deep down in my spirit that it was true. Sigh...

When you love and look up to the person who is the Jezebel. When you love the abuser and endure the manipulating control because it makes you feel useful and needed. When you believe that the pain of sacrifice is going to yield a great anointing. This was all me.

Deep down within the pit of my spirit, I knew it was there. I've been like a deer on the tracks with a freight train coming. Just standing there, except someone has pushed me out the way. Yeah, I knew this, but I just did not have a name for it. The mandatory meetings, seeds, conferences, workshops and guilt-ridden attendances each one I felt pressured to attend, as well as scared not to attend. The days I was almost afraid to get out of my bed because I was cursed. Gripped with fear and dread that was going to befall me because I had missed a tithe to pay the mortgage. Always trying to please, measure up, be obedient, serve, commit, and connect. IT just never thought that IT would ever get exposed. Well…IT did. There are some truths within us that we know all too well and we love to see them surface. And then, there are those truths which we try to hide and avoid.

But the light of truth will eventually expose everything, especially when you flip the switch. My lights are beginning to flicker. This religious spirit had to go.

## Change

I am making some moves and making changes. There has to be more than what I have experienced. There is something that I am looking for, something that my spirit seems to be craving. Now for it to be craving something, evidently it must be something that my spirit once had and knows about all too well. Hmm…it is almost as if my spirit knows, but is waiting for my flesh to catch on. We can only crave something that we've once had. At some point in my beginning, I had what I am now longing for. My spirit knew and my spirit knows. Kingdom? Was I once part of this grand Kingdom?

# The Helen Keller Moment

Helen Keller was born sometime in the early 1800s. Around the age of 19 months, she became very ill and developed a fever so high that she became blind and deaf. At this age she was just beginning to talk, but the fever left her in a world of silence and darkness, unable to communicate. Can you imagine not being able to hear, see, or speak? Which one do you think is the worst? Not seeing or not hearing? Helen Keller said, "The problems of deafness are deeper and more complex, if not more important, than those of blindness. Deafness is a much worse misfortune. For it means the loss of the most vital stimulus — the sound of the voice that brings language, sets thoughts astir and keeps us in the intellectual company of man. Blindness cuts us off from things, but deafness cuts us off from people."

Although she could not see, hear, or speak, everything that she needed was within her. It was dormant in a state darkness and silence. I likened myself to Helen Keller per say. There was a time when I felt as if I were blind in a seeing world. I had trouble seeing what so many around me saw. Someone

would say "Man of God..." and I was like –*where*? I was
deaf to certain things too. Things would fly across the pulpit
and I would look around seeing many partaking of it, while I
could not comprehend it at all. Everywhere I turned, it
seemed that others were hearing from God and all I heard was
silence. Helen's teacher, Anne Sullivan, would spell words
into Helen's hand and she would spell them back only
thinking that it was a game, not comprehending what was
going on. She would spell D-O-L-L and hand her a doll, but
Helen was not able to connect the word DOLL to the actual
doll. You see, that is what religion does. The Holy Ghost kept
spelling it out right in my hand, and I responded on auto pilot,
not comprehending the truth behind it. A form of godliness.

On one particular afternoon, Anne Sullivan took Helen Keller
out to the well to draw water. As she drew the water, she
spelled the word W-A-T-E-R into Helen's hand as the cool
liquid ran over Helen's other hand. This was the moment that
the lights came on. There was a connection. She knew...she
just knew that the word that Anne was spelling in her hand
was that cool liquid running over her hand. At that point
Helen's soul rekindled a memory and deep within her

atrophic throat muscles came a word that she had not muttered since the age of 19 months. The word was "wha wha", meaning water. It was at that moment that Helen knew what water was! Water was "Wha, wha!" Everything from that point had a meaning and her discovery into a new world had begun. She ran to the tree and Annie spelled T-R-E-E. She dropped to the ground and Annie spelled G-R-O-U-N-D. This was the day her soul recognized the unseen world.

I believe that I am on the verge of my Helen Keller moment. I believe that I am going to go to the well and as the spirit begins to flow, something is going connect and all the pieces, all the "letters" are going to begin to fit. As I cry for help, I believe that H-E-L-P is here. My eyes are going to begin seeing into a realm that I have never experienced before: my ears will hear like never before and even my speech will be different. Like Helen, I am going to get that missing connect and a whole new world is going to open up before me. My hands are open, my heart is open, my mind is open, I am completely surrendering to HIM.

## Detoxing

Boy oh boy… when you truly begin to seek the Kingdom;
meaning that you slough off all of your religious expectations
and doctrinal rituals and dive into HIS word, you can begin to
truly see yourself spiritually. You see, I have decided to take
this journey and for me, I am calling it a religious detox! Yes,
a detox. I was beginning to feel constipated with so much
religious junk that I could barely sleep at night. I am not
kidding. This was my religious breakdown! And that is the
problem with religion, it breaks you down and sucks the life
out of you. Religion always asks for more and that was what I
was trying to do. More! I did more reading and studying,
more prayer time, more worship, more classes, more
programs, more conferences, more accountability, more
church attendance, more seeds sown, and more volunteering.
I did more, more, and then some more. And if I wasn't doing
more, I felt guilty for not doing more. To be honest, I felt like
a failure because I could not keep up with the "Mores". In
some form or fashion, I would fail at trying to do more, or I
would feel convicted because my whole heart was not
involved. Sometimes even doing things grudgingly which

would of course, you guessed it, cause me to repent and pray more! And not that anyone forced me to do these rituals. It was my own perception and decades of twisted doctrines laced with traditions that I set as "My Law". At times I felt as if I was losing my mind. But, worse than that, I had begun to fear that maybe I was not truly saved. My logic told me that there was no way I could be saved and feel the way that I was feeling. I kept on telling myself that somehow, some way I had allowed myself to get demonized again and I had to get free. So, the first thing that I had to do was shut everything down. I decided to do a complete system reboot, so to speak. I went back to the origin of my salvation which is Jesus Christ and I clang onto HIM for my sanity. The mindset that I had was a stronghold, yet I yearned for the Father. I wanted a relationship with Jesus and I wanted to be led by the Holy Ghost. Therefore, everyone else and everything, including the institutional church, had to wait. I needed to repent, and I did. I repented for being on autopilot with God, and for placing religion over relationship. I threw-out all of my religious "junk" and doctrines, and simply asked the Father to allow me to start all over. I began this journey detoxing mentally, physically, and spiritually. The only one on board was my spirit man. Flesh was screaming inside throwing tantrums as if it were saying, "You ARE going to listen to me!" My soul and emotions were telling me once more, "You are on your own, lady." It was only in my spirit that I heard, deep down amongst all the junk saying, "I am willing and I want to do it". And so, it begins with Matthew 6:33 (KJV), "Seek ye first the Kingdom of God and his righteousness; and all these things will be added." I began right there. Now, I really did not know what the Kingdom was, but I decided that I was going to seek it. I believed that if I went looking for it, then either I would find it, or it would find me. I even started praying from a primal position. I began simply saying the Lord's prayer daily. That prayer had everything I needed in it. Even the first two words created a change within me; "Our Father". My religious boundaries always had me calling Him, God! I saw Him as the great distant God, who was always pissed-off at me. Now, I was beginning to draw near to HIM as Father.

*Matthew 6:33 (KJV): "Seek ye first the Kingdom of God and His righteousness and everything you need will be added to you*"…is where I am right now, and I am going to stay here for a minute. According to this scripture, if I just seek the Kingdom first, everything else I need will line up down the road. So, off I am on this journey to really comprehend what the Kingdom of God is really about. These days it seems to be a buzz word within the religious community; yet when I began my search, I found that all Jesus preached was Kingdom! My search also led me to the fact that just within the four gospels, Jesus mentioned Kingdom over 67 times. This is what I have found: Kingdom is defined as "a country, region or realm that is dominated by a King". So, what Kingdom was Jesus talking about? *John 18:36 (NLT), Jesus tells that "My Kingdom is not an earthly Kingdom. If it were, my followers would fight to keep me from being handed over to the Jewish leaders.* Here is the ESV translation: *"Jesus answered, My kingdom is not of this world. If my kingdom were of this world, my servants would have been fighting, that I might not be delivered over to the Jews."*

His Kingdom represents HIS culture. My lesson number one: I have to blot out everything except the HOLY SPIRIT AND THE WORD OF GOD, and I MUST make seeking the

Kingdom my number one priority. I was wondering how to do this. I mean, I can come up with some spiritual steps but as I pondered over this lesson, a practical example popped in my head as well.

Let's assume you are in debt and your house and car has been depleted, as well as your pantry. What would be your first priority to acquire these necessities? Employment. A job! You would begin doing everything you could to find employment. You would begin to "seek" for it, you would prepare for it, you would study for it if you had to. Even what you wear would become relative to you seeking employment. Your first thought in the morning and your last thought in the evening would be all about seeking employment. And once a call came in, you would then prepare for the interview. Now, you will pull out that blue power suit, clean up, shave, sleek the hair back, and get ready. No matter what, you will make it to the interview and again why? Because you are seeking employment. Then, let's say you get the dream job. Now, you become part of the company. Immediately, you begin to adapt to the culture of the company. If everyone in the office wear a tie, then you would begin wearing a tie. If they all break for lunch at noon, then you would follow suit. If the office is basically quiet and reserve, then you too would become quiet and reserved. I bet you would even whisper during private calls. If everyone is expected to work overtime, then you would work overtime. You would also become familiar with the company's bylaws and rules. You will probably be required to read the manual, which is a book on how to reap the benefits of being employed, as well as the do's and don'ts. And now in return for your being employed as a representative for the company, you are paid. The owner or chief of the company gives you a check, and with that check you can now regain your necessities. And so, you buy a car...why? Because you need a car to get to work. You buy a house...why? Because you need shelter. You fill your pantry up with food? Why? Because you to need to eat in order to live. By being a part of this company and being employed, you are able to acquire the basic necessities. Now, let's also imagine that in time you receive promotions due to your commitment and submission to this company. You can now begin to bless others; you may buy additional things or properties. In other words, things become added because you made seeking employment a priority!

I have to seek the Kingdom like the one great pearl. As I have been born again, I am now an ambassador and thus, I must set out to learn more of my Kingdom and culture. I am desperately seeking employment in the Kingdom! I know He pays well.

## This Religious Demon Ain't No Joke! At Least For Me It Ain't

The departure from religion is almost like a death. It is all I've known. The protocols, rituals, and traditions are what I believed were how one ushered in the presence of God. I have to be honest, I miss it. Right now, I feel so alone and segregated. I just want to go somewhere and weep. This religious system is like a drug. You become addicted to it to get your high and once you realize what it has done to you, you begin to hate the very thing that you crave. Just being brutally honest here. I feel like I am losing my mind. Deep down, I believe that some aspects of this system are wrong. Yet, I feel the need to continue doing them. Isn't this called insanity? I have built a system of relationships all centered around church and it has become my identity. Help me, Holy Ghost! Lead me to the TRUTH. If I am demonized, then please expose it. I wave the flag...I am so done right now. I only have one scripture to grab and claw my fingers into the seam, so that I cannot let it go.

Matthew 6:33, "Seek ye first the Kingdom of God and His righteousness..." Okay God...Okay, I am seeking.

# Reality Is Setting In

Something within me is beginning to change. As I sat in the congregation tonight, waiting for the predicted as well as scheduled praise and worship performance, I saw some members of the team begin to flip the switch and turn on. As soon as the mic was placed in a hand and the live music began the intro, the show began. They had the primers. The ones to prime the pump so to speak, and they sounded great! They jumped and sang, gave instructions for me to raise my hands, close my eyes, and tell Jesus how great HE is. Some gave Him adorations and continued to sing with all they had in them, while others were clearly focused on keeping the right notes and maintaining the harmony. As I watched them perform, I saw all kinds of faces. Some were smiling and really trying to get us to engage, a few were in their own world of praise, while some faces showed aching feet and tired bodies. I found myself going along with the motions and instructions, until I caught myself. This is not about anyone, but the King. I closed my eyes and began to focus on HIM and HIM alone. Not the team, but HIM. He is King of Kings and is worthy of every ounce of worship. But it must be in spirit and in truth.

I wonder, why do we have to prime people to praise the King of Kings? Is it because we have become so accustomed to a religious way of doing things that we now have become convinced that the only way to usher in the "the presence" is written down on some itinerary? We have timelines for worship. It's amazing how we are told that this is "worship" and it should be all about HIM, yet it is the time when you will see leaders and others talking, walking, catching up on the hellos and even complementing one's shoes. It is a social time where we capture moments of the worship in between being told to move down a seat or looking around the sanctuary. But yet, when the Pastor walks in, everyone stops what they are doing. We cut the conversation short, we tell the toddler to shush, and we stand for the man and clap while we socialized when it was about the "King". Do we have it twisted here?

I remember once, the Pastor of this church was running late, so one of the Elders asked if anyone had a testimony to share. A young woman excitedly raised her hand and was beckoned to stand and share. She began telling her story, clearly nervous, but yet excited and eager to let everyone know of the miracle that had occurred in her life. I must say it was a faith builder! A fascinating testimony of faith and just about everyone in the room was glued to her words, when all of a sudden, the Pastor came walking through the door. The Elder immediately, in the midst of this lady's testimonial, motioned everyone to stand and clap to receive the "Man of God". The poor lady was silenced. I recall thinking how sad it was to realize that she was just a filler. Fluff to fill time until the Pastor arrived. Her testimony, although powerful and dear to her, meant nothing to that leader. But that is one of the tentacles of religion; it keeps time. It has to. This spirit cannot afford to allow the Holy Spirit to flow, otherwise, it would become exposed and get cast down.

## Scurr'd To Pray

Have you ever had prayer anxiety? I have. You know where
we are given the mic to pray for a certain amount of time, and
then the Pastor or First Lady is running late, so the intercessor
or prayer squad leader signals you to keep it going. You now
find yourself praying for the city, state, America, nations,
Israel, the world, the galaxy and solar system. Next, you are
now pulling down strongholds, and serving notice on the
enemy, you pray for the schools, marketplace... anywhere or
anyone, trying to "kill time". Then, once the leader arrives,
you get the "cut it" signal. God forbid you keep praying...
then, you would be told you are out of order.

## Coming Around The Corner

For years, I made them all icons. I worshipped my leaders and I thought that they were to be adored, obeyed, and loved from a distance.

Did you know that there is a book on it? There is a book on how to treat the elite leaders and how to keep quiet in their presence, not to invoke conversations, and how we are not to look a Bishop in the eye and folks, I fell for it all. I was afraid to look at them for fear of breaking a religious code. Is this really of God? To make sure that we address each leader with the correct title and treat them differently? No. But I was one who cut family vacations just to serve. I sucked it up when a leader would snap at me, treat me rudely or hurt my feelings assuming that I was suffering for Christ by their rebuke. I gave endlessly simply because I was asked to. I can go on...But let me say this...I forgave everyone and I forgive myself. This is not about what was done to me, but what I allowed to be done to me, mainly by people who believe that they were showing love and guiding me. Warning: If you ever decide to let go of religion and begin to seek HIM...as your eyes begin to open, you will see the ugliness of it all. You will also begin to see the demons involved. If you can relate to what I am saying and feel revengeful or even angry, stop now. Check your spirit and get your character in check. But if it makes you sad, know that you are turning a corner.

## When They Say One Thing and Do Another

God knows I do not agree with some of the things going on with my leadership... however, 1 Peter 2:17 (ESV) says to, "Honor everyone. Love the brotherhood. Fear God. Honor the emperor."

I shall do that. However, I will no longer support major projects or endeavors unless it is validated that what I am sacrificing and giving towards will be used for that SAID purpose. For example, you as my leader say we are going to build a library. I get excited about the library. Extremely. I sacrifice and sow joyfully into the library. When you talk about its purpose, I stand and clap and get excited. After all, this is my library too. I am collecting and buying books to donate to the library. You share about how it will be used for the glory of God and I even begin preparing for the great things that will happen in our library. But then, you build an event center with a skating rink. I am disappointed, but don't say anything because I cannot question you. I get over my feelings and so I decide to volunteer and help out with the center. Yet, I cringe to hear how much you charge those who "built" it to use it. If you reserve the right to use the tithes, offerings and gifts to do as deemed by the church or trustee board, then why bother to tell the congregation at all? Why tell me that my child will have somewhere to skate and that they will serve ice cream, when the truth is that the building is seldomly open because you want the place to run just off of volunteers. Between church and work, most people's days are full. Who wants to volunteer on their only day off?! Give a teenager or a widow some extra cash. Volunteers. Yet you charge an outrageous fee for my kids to skate! And to top it off, the ice cream maker stays broken?! Nope. No more. Call me Petty Patty right now. Done.

## I Hope This Helps

I joined a fasting/prayer group, which to this day I believe
was God ordained. Again, my flesh acted like it was
punishing me. My soul still keeps telling me,
"Gurrrrrrl...You are on ya' own", but my spirit kept thriving
for truth and a relationship with the one true God of all. My
Father. Last night...I had trouble sleeping.

# A Set Back

What do you do when you begin to feel that everything you've been told and perceived to be in the word of God is not true? Some on these beliefs were part of my foundation, and I am totally crushed and confused. I feel like a child that has been kept inside the house for twenty years. For years I was told that if I went outside, the sunlight would burn me...that the rain would make me melt and that the wind would sweep me away. Imagine believing something like this only to find out that the sun does not burn, the rain actually feels great, and the wind is refreshing. Father, I do not want to die and go to hell based on a false doctrine. I am almost afraid to read my Bible...because what if I read it and misinterpret something. I feel like I am losing my mind. Everyone claims to be an expert. Everyone claims to have the answers. I am crying right now...seeing arguments over doctrines and both sides sound right! I kind of want to run back into my religious strongholds. At least there I felt like I was Heaven bound...at least there I had someone to talk to. All I can do is start all over...Genesis chapter one.

## It Is Getting Harder For Me

It is getting harder for me as I embark on receiving the
revelation of the Kingdom. It has become very difficult to
look at some churches the same. I went to my church. I was
greeted and really glad to see everyone. I love my church
family. I mean I really love them. I can see a few faces in my
mind as I type this and I am serious, I love the members of
"Blank". Anyway, I got there just in time for praise and
"Entertainment" again. You know how it goes, two fast songs
and two slow songs. Sometimes three or the extended version,
if the Pastor is running a bit late. What I wished though was
that I had missed the offering sermon. Why do we have to
have a fifteen-minute sermon on tithes and offering? I can
guarantee you that 99% of the people have already
determined what they were going to give or hopefully, some
have simply asked the Holy Spirit what they should
give. Sometimes these sermons kind of make me a bit
embarrassed. One time it got so bad that I felt like I was
about to crawl up under my seat. I looked at my pocketbook
and it was bent all over as if it were frowning. All creased
and just a sagging as if it too, was tired and fed up with the

money sermons. I am sure some folks out in the congregation went back into their pocketbooks and gave more that day. He scared them really. Telling them that they would be cursed with a curse. Well, here is a shocker for you…I don't believe that. I used to be scared like that. But not anymore. I don't struggle with giving in fear like I used to, yet I give now probably more than I ever did. To be honest, after truly learning about tithing, I now do not believe that it is biblical for today. I AM AMAZED THAT I SAID THAT. But let me say a disclaimer for those of you who are ready to cast me into hell. If you sign a membership agreement to give 10% of your income to your local church, then you SHOULD DO IT. Treat it the same way as if you were part of an organization or club. You pay the dues, right? I have found through the years that when it comes to giving in some churches, it appears that the rules have changed or I guess new revelations have surfaced to make the believer keep up with the rising cost of running a church. For example, back in the eighties I was told that it was acceptable to tithe on your net income, then in the nineties, I guess God changed His mind because I was then told that I needed to tithe on my gross income. The millennial brought in more elaborate offerings such as seed offerings, sacrificial offerings, first fruit offerings, love offerings, offerings where you give one day's pay, a week's pay, and even a month's offering! Nothing wrong with any of them I *guess,* if you want to pay it. I think it is great to give. But I do not believe in saying that people are going to be cursed if they do not give...nor do I believe that it takes money to seal a blessing. I find it refreshing to be in services where there is no pressure to give. I tend to want to give more. I despise money lines too. Every time I ever gave in a money line, I felt pressured and by having to walk up there in front of everyone, I would feel sick to my stomach. And then, at times when I did not have it to give, I still would feel bad. I would sit in my seat feeling terrible about the new dress I had bought or the family meal we splurged on. Now, I give and I give cheerfully to several ministries...plural. I also love to be a blessing to others. I am also careful about where and what I sow into. Also, I now refuse to sow into any more of those pyramid conferences or buy into these visions that do not happen. Enough on money.

## Titles To The Head

What have we created? Titles, titles, titles...they seem to have gone to our heads. Shaking my own head. To hear a Bishop's wife proclaim that the laity is not on the same level because of her title almost made me cry. "We are not on the same level." Well, is she correct?

You know, I am not sure if I can find enough of the words, phrases, and adjectives to describe the glory and honor expected to be given to some Pastors and their wives. And please let's not forget the Archbishop Deluxe to whom I would not be able to look directly in the eye. I wonder would a gentle whelp in a high-pitched key of "C" be received as appropriate for such an elite soul. Whether they pastor five or five thousand, there seems to be this invisible halo hovering above some heads. I guess this is the church age that we live in where titles of Bishop and Apostle are popping up everywhere you look. Yet, the Bible says that The Son of God "made Himself of no reputation" (Philippians 2:7, KJV). The Bible says that the greatest among you would serve. I am so confused, because I am seeing people ordained as a Bishop with a hand full of members and if I were to ask some Apostles about their church plants, they would direct me to the peace lilies by the pulpit. This breeds a non-biblical separation between the robes and the rayon. Yet, I hear and see this often, how we, the laity are not on the same level and treated as such. Can you imagine serving and watching the leaders eat while you stand in primed position against the wall with your hands folded neatly in front of you, as your tummy growls from hunger pangs? Oh, you will eat, but you will eat last and you will eat "out of site". WHAT DOES THIS SOUND LIKE?

Matthew 23:11-12, ESV
*The greatest among you will be your servant. For whoever exalts himself will be humbled, and whoever humbles himself will be exalted.*

Romans 12:16, NIV
*Live in harmony with one another. Do not be proud, but be willing to associate with people of low position. Do not be conceited.*

<u>1 Corinthians 13:4, NIV</u>

*Love is patient, love is kind. It does not envy, it does not boast, it is not proud.*

## The Jerk

Matthew 18:3 instructs me to change and be like a little child. And it says that unless I do that, I will never enter the Kingdom of Heaven. Wow! So, guess what? I am making an exchange to change. Today, I resume throwing out my theologies, perceptions, a few handbooks, doctrine manuals and even some best sellers, all are going out of my mental door! Give me the primer per say. I need to start on the beginner level. Remember when it was as simple as: See God work, see God move. God said go. God said stop. God loves you. God loves me.

I come as a child with no perceived formalities. Maybe that is the position we need to get back to. The primal position. Let's go back to the beginning and learn it all over again. Our American alphabet is the basis of our communication, as well as comprehension of how to live in the U.S.A. Imagine if we treated the Bible like that. Except you be a little child...Wow, this really got me thinking. My mind went back to when I had just gotten saved and witnessed the aftermath of the death of a small child. The child had gotten hit by a car and his lifeless body was lying literally in the middle street. It was an emotional scene for both the mother and the young woman who had hit the child. I was with my former mentor at the time. We were both in college, but she was more "mature" in the Lord than I and for all accounts, many of us on campus looked up to her and tried to model after her walk, as well as seek her for Godly wisdom. I on the other hand had just gotten saved. I can still see the child lying in the street, I can still remember the clothes he had on. I looked at my mentor, grabbed her hand and said, "Let's go pray for him" and I began to step towards the scene. My mentor grabbed me and quickly jerked me back, as I had already taken about two steps ahead of her. As I looked at her, she sternly told me, "No, you can't do that! You gotta be led by the Holy Ghost, you just don't go praying for people." With all my questioning, there was no further explanation. One of the first rules of doctrine was not to question leadership or usurp authority, and so right there I became a spectator like everyone else. Was this childlike faith? Yes, I was a babe in Christ, newly saved for about two months; but, at this point all I knew was that Jesus raised the dead and that He was a healer, so I logically and to some foolishly thought...Why not?!! I did not know about protocols, getting approvals, or fear of failing at this time. I was a babe with childlike faith. All I knew was that Jesus did it and I was going to do it, but instead I got jerked back. I know now that my mentor did what she thought was for my good, reputation, and discipleship. After all, I was a neophyte to all of this, and I had to be taught not to be so zealous and to wait on the guidance from the Holy Spirit. Right? But this jerk, jerked more than my hand. It was my first jerk into the world of "Religious Order and Protocols". What if it had been the Holy Spirit pulling me to pray for the child? Had his spirit not returned back into his body, I would have not thought any less of God being a healer. I would not have had one iota of embarrassment. My logic would have been that "I am going to keep going and believing until the miracle comes". Like the lepers. To every man is dealt the measure of faith. I wonder if we all could begin with this great childlike dead raising faith, but then it gets tainted by religious adult faith, which in turn diminishes the formation of miracle movements. We get programmed into thinking that only certain elites within the church can ever attempt certain acts, religion tells us that we are not spiritual enough, that we don't pray enough, fast enough, read the Bible enough. It tells us that for some, even after decades, we have not reached our maturity in the Lord to attempt to do such things. Religion says that I must be close to being perfect, I have to fast more, pray more, read more, build platforms, and earn a title. Religion tells us, "One day, I am going to raise the dead". While Kingdom says, "Now is the time to raise the dead." This jerk has held me for 30 years and it has been nurtured by many more jerks. After years of salvation, I still felt the jerk. It had become apparent again while I was standing in the hospital room of one of my dearest friends. She had just died. There were about twenty people in this room. The family, Pastors, Leaders, Prophets, Ministers, and probably all of the five-fold ministry times four. We joined hands, we prayed, and we cried. But I must admit to you today, that my tears were not for the loss of my friend, instead my tears were because as I looked at all of the power standing in that room, no one…not one person suggested that we pray her back to life. Maybe it crossed the minds of a couple of us in there. I just know that I was disgusted with myself for being such a coward and not saying anything, and worst yet, I was in fear of being rebuked. I felt that we had let her down per say. Amazing how we will pull on the medical experts to try every last thing in the book to prolong life, yet some of us are so slow to pray for healing; to pray for life. This is a stronghold of the mind.

I remember having a conversation about a well-known Pastor who had died and a few of the younger congregants were attempting to find his body and pray for his resurrection. There was a whole lot of jerking going on, as well as some rebukes toward those ironically "young saints" who were rallying for a miracle. Mentors were forced to "Have a talk with them". Leaders had to quickly squash this movement before it got out of hand. In this instance, the strength of our stronghold/mindset prevailed, whereas to a child, to pray with expectation would have been the norm.

I was told that years ago in a remote village in Africa, of a people who were walking on water! When asked about how and why, all they knew to say was, "Because Jesus did." I remember when the discussion was going on about the Pastor

who had died, someone made a statement that they thought
would cease the conversations; "Well his body has been
embalmed now so there is no way he can be raised from the
dead." This statement coming from a well-seasoned saint
took me back for a moment. I remember looking at her and
could literally see that she had her faith within a border. I
wanted to ask her, "Do you really think that Formaldehyde,
which God made anyway, can keep the resurrection power of
Jesus from raising the dead?" I remained silent. My thoughts
about this beloved Pastor were simple. My questions were:
Are we ready for this? It is not that WE CANNOT RAISE
THE DEAD, but are we mature in Christ enough to handle
the repercussions from such a miracle? Will we give HIM
glory within the media frenzy? Can you handle the religious
groupies who will now come and follow *you*? Such a miracle
will create one of the greatest and highest platforms many
have ever seen. There would be monuments, statues, and
pilgrimages. Along with the glory will come character
defamation, accusations, and life changes that would surface
because of an another "Lazarus" miracle. My opinion is this:
Many in the western religious sect are not ready to handle

such an event. But guess who is? Those as little children who have entered the Kingdom of God. Knowing their citizenship, authority, and King, these children can handle it. They can handle it because in the Kingdom, such is expected and always anticipated. All that they know is what God says. The system of the world does not apply to them and when they hear the language of religion, doubt, fear, and excuses, just like a visitor in a foreign land, they do not understand. They have a simple, powerful faith and trust in the Great God Almighty.

## Getting My Mind Out Of My Mind!

Sometimes you have to get your mind out of mind! The more I learn truth and seek the Kingdom of God, the more I too despise religion. Today, my main focus is practicing ways to renew my mind. As I started to draw near to God, I began to see myself for what I was. I did not like what I saw. My character needed an overhaul. My sight had become distorted, so to speak.

## Keeping My Stance

I spent today focusing on seeing myself before the Great God Almighty. The first thing that I did I dreaded, and that was facing my issues. You know, the ones that we ignore and do not want to face? I faced them head-on, and on this day, I began to work on them. I also began to work on my character, attitudes, and emotions. Was it easy? No, and again, I say NO! But God will meet you at the intersection of your desire to change. And even though all my prayers, declarations, and efforts did not appear to bring immediate changes, I kept my confession and I kept my stance.


## Last Night

I slept last night.

## Not As Easy As It Sounds

A stronghold is a mindset. And I have a stronghold. I am
going to keep trying until I have victory over this!! I knew
that my mindset had to change. Today, again I focus on
Romans 12:2 (KJV) *"And be not conformed to this world:
but be ye transformed by the renewing of your mind, that ye
may prove what is that good, and acceptable, and perfect, will
of God."* A few days ago, I began the process of cleaning out
my mental file cabinet. All mental files that I could not back-
up with the word of God concerning salvation, worship or
Christianity went into what I call my trash pile. This was a
hard task. Let me be honest right here. Some of these files I
wanted to hold on to. They had been in my possession for
over 42 years. I mean this is how I was raised to do church.
Some of these ideologies were how I was taught to do in
order to usher in the presence of God and saturate the
atmosphere. These protocols were ordained for how we
sanctified ourselves and walked holy before the Lord.
Included in this pile were instructions on how to pray, what to
say, what to do, what not to say, what to wear and when to
wear it. Files on how to worship, how to hear from God, what

was permissible and what was not. A few times I battled with thoughts like: "What if I throw out the wrong file? What are the saints of the grand ole church going to say? Worst yet, what if I get sat down?" I was bombarded with many mental lassos looping me back and forth, trying to stop me from cleaning out the trash; but, I kept going and I asked the Father to stop me if I was going too fast, or if I was being emotional or operating in error. Y'all, it was hard, and at times I cried. Can you imagine throwing out what you thought was your very foundation for living? I could visually see my mind throwing out file after file of religious doctrines and habits. To be honest, I had a hard time letting go of some of these strongholds, but I had to create my own ground zero and build back up. The first step of rebuilding was to make sure that my foundation was solid. I sought the Holy Spirit and my prayer was very simple, but sincere: "Lead and guide me to the Truth." The breakdown began. This detoxing is not easy.

## I Ain't Sayin' Nuthin'!

Since I've been back, I have only shared my experience and
what was told to me to only a select few. A very select
few. One person in particular just looked at me when I
shared, and the look in her eyes was like she was crying for
help as she listened. Oddly, she never said a word. I hope she
doesn't throw me under the bus. I have also been approached
by a few people who act like I am in some type of secret
society. To my surprise though, there are a few who
acknowledged similar feelings as I did and claim that they
feel controlled and spiritually abused. Okay let me say this, I
ain't falling for it! The last time I opened up my heart to a
couple of people about my struggles and how I was feeling, a
meeting was called and I was rebuked by a leader for
speaking against leadership. I was threatened to be dismissed
or sat down in the 60-day corner. So nope! I ain't saying
nothing! I will get through this by myself and with the help of
the HOLY GHOST!

## I Feel So Lonely

Now, I will try to explain it if I can. But as I am going through this "detoxing", I feel very lonely. Sometimes it is evident that the Father is all I got. I got no one, but I kinda feel that this is exactly where He wants me. He wanted me to get to know Him as Father. So, I am spending the day focusing on HIM as FATHER and not as God.

## Religion

Merriam Webster defines *religion* as: "A personal set or institutionalized system of religious attitudes, beliefs, and practices." I can concur with that. However, I also believe that there is a demonic spirit of religion, the same spirit that Jesus had to address in Matthew, chapter 23. Jesus came down hard on religion.

Matthew 23:1-3 (MSG): "Now Jesus turned to address his disciples, along with the crowd that had gathered with them. The religion scholars and Pharisees are competent teachers in God's Law. You won't go wrong in following their teachings on Moses. But be careful about following *them*. They talk a good line, but they don't live it. They don't take it into their hearts and live it out in their behavior. It's all spit-and-polish veneer."

4-7: "Instead of giving you God's Law as food and drink by which you can banquet on God, they package it in bundles of rules, loading you down like pack animals. They seem to take pleasure in watching you stagger under these loads, and wouldn't think of lifting a finger to help. Their lives are perpetual fashion shows, embroidered prayer shawls one day and flowery prayers the next. They love to sit at the head table at church dinners, basking in the most prominent positions, preening in the radiance of public flattery, receiving honorary degrees, and getting called 'Doctor' and 'Reverend'."

8-10: "Don't let people do that to *you*, put you on a pedestal like that. You all have a single Teacher, and you are all classmates. Don't set people up as experts over your life, letting them tell you what to do. Save that authority for God; let *him* tell you what to do. No one else should carry the title of 'Father'; you have only one Father, and he's in heaven. And don't let people maneuver you into taking charge of them. There is only one Life-Leader for you and them— Christ."

11-12: "Do you want to stand out? Then step down. Be a servant. If you puff yourself up, you'll get the wind knocked out of you. But if you're content to simply be yourself, your life will count for plenty."

13: "I've had it with you! You're hopeless, your religion scholars, you Pharisees! Frauds! Your lives are roadblocks to

God's kingdom. You refuse to enter, and won't let anyone else in either."

15: "You're hopeless, you religion scholars and Pharisees! Frauds! You go halfway around the world to make a convert, but once you get him you make him into a replica of yourselves, double-damned."

16-22: "You're hopeless! What arrogant stupidity! You say, 'If someone makes a promise with his fingers crossed, that's nothing; but if he swears with his hand on the Bible, that's serious.' What ignorance! Does the leather on the Bible carry more weight than the skin on your hands? And what about this piece of trivia: 'If you shake hands on a promise, that's nothing; but if you raise your hand that God is your witness, that's serious'? What ridiculous hairsplitting! What difference does it make whether you shake hands or raise hands? A promise is a promise. What difference does it make if you make your promise inside or outside a house of worship? A promise is a promise. God is present, watching and holding you to account regardless."

23-24: "You're hopeless, your religion scholars and Pharisees! Frauds! You keep meticulous account books, tithing on every nickel and dime you get, but on the meat of God's Law, things like fairness and compassion and commitment—the absolute basics! —you carelessly take it or leave it. Careful bookkeeping is commendable, but the basics are required. Do you have any idea how silly you look, writing a life story that's wrong from start to finish, nitpicking over commas and semicolons?"

Whew! See what I mean? Jesus hated this religious system and He did not sugarcoat it either. Therefore, as I continue on this journey to break free and walk into my Kingdom assignment. I must fight to stay focused. First and foremost, you cannot fight religion with religion, therefore, I have to complete my process of detoxification. This chapter though…Mathew 23. Wow! I never really realized how much He despised the religious system. So now, I wonder why do we do it? The rules, the elaborate vestments, clown suits, shawls, special seating and titles…and selective serving?!

You could probably knock me over with a flower if I ever saw certain First Ladies frying chicken, or the Bishop cleaning the bathroom. I am sure many of them once did. Anyway, going to read this chapter again.

## It Is Hard To Let Go!

Well, I had a setback! My phone was beeping with demands and I again felt the religious pull. I gave in. I obligated myself like I've done so many times before and yet in my heart, I dreaded it. To do what I agreed to do was like taking my heart and eating it like a rotten potato. So, why did I agree to this? Because religion compelled me to be there. It compelled me to dress the part and it compelled me to be obedient to my call. I did not believe that the event was Kingdom work; but yet, out of feeling compelled and fearful of the repercussions of what would happen if I just said no. Again, I found myself in a familiar place, where I felt pushed and forced to participate. Again, I found myself having the familiar sick feeling, tearing up and feeling like I was losing my mind. I hated religion and how it feasted on sucking the life out of you, yet I grabbed some files from off of the trash pile; and that night I went to sleep feeling defeated.

## You Tie A Knot and Hang On

*And be not conformed to this world: but be ye transformed by the renewing of your mind, that ye may prove what is that good, and acceptable, and perfect, will of God. Romans 12:2 (KJV)*

I had a lot of disappointments recently. But this morning, I got up with a greater expectation and declarations:

- I am going to continue with the detox, and I will overcome this religious pull on my life.
- I am determined to Love as He loves and Live as He lives.
- I will not be critical of or condescending to those who are still embedded in religion as I begin to study more and more about the Kingdom of God.
- I will not be a coward or tolerant for what I believe to be Truth.
- I am going to stop dumb-downing myself for the sake of religious people.
- When I have setbacks, I will not beat up myself. I will rev-up and go forth.

## Chicken and Peas Will Make You Sneeze

Getting off of Facebook for a while. I am so grieved. So many posts seem to always be on the defense, playing the victim or trying to prove subliminal points to a specific group. And most of these are from Pastors. And then there are the countless posts from leaders who, regardless of what they say, are "groupies" to latch on and say "Amen, First Lady!" or "Say it Pastor!" I believe that some of these people could say, "Chicken and peas will make you sneeze" and within seconds, someone will "LIKE" it and comment "Preach!" This makes me so sad. It really does. The religious remarks, the demands. The words "Honor, Submit, and Obey" always seems to find their way in my social media threads. I wonder why? I have no problem with submitting or being obedient to God. Obedience is worship! I believe in accountability. I do have a problem with being manipulated and controlled. I believe in being respectful to leadership. I believe in keeping them informed, especially if they are depending upon my services. It is not fair to not inform them that you will not be present when you have agreed to be there, and you know that they may be depending on you. That is not fair to them or anyone for that matter. But to be told "No", I cannot visit a friend's church if I want to. To be told "No", I cannot pray for a person in need without the consent of an Elder. To be told "No", I cannot attend a conference, a dance recital, or take vacation during a big conference or convocation…that is not submission. That is control. When it comes to leadership, some of our leaders are poor examples. They dictate, but they do not relate at all, nor do we ever see them serving. I tell you what, if I saw some First Ladies even picking up tissue from off the floor after service, my jaw would drop.

## Alone

As I begin to detox, I am noticing that religion is becoming appalling to me; yet, it is difficult for me. I truly feel like I am so alone. I am not taking any of the Xanax that was prescribed to me. I refuse. I was given 20 pills and I still have 20 pills. Religion will not push me to the pill.

## Feeling So Defeated Today

I would say that I've had a meltdown. I guess the first of the year brings all of these religious acts, and because I decided not to participate this time, I cannot help but think that I am doing something wrong. I completed these Daniel fasts for years and for the most part, I did it because my church required it of me and not because the Father told me to, or I felt the urge or need to fast. I actually did it with an attitude. I dreaded it and all I could think about was the end date. I am ashamed to admit that even the corporate prayer did not go well for me either. You show up and everyone is scattered about in a seat with soft music playing. I sat, I prayed for people, I prayed for myself...and after 15 minutes, I was getting sleepy. I was not the only one! I felt like a heathen, just sitting there secretly staring at my phone while others were "praying". This went on for almost a full hour. Wow...I wonder if my 15-minute prayer is unworthy. Does it show weakness on my part? After the one hour of silently praying and sleeping, a minister got up to speak. They shared a topic for about 15 minutes.

Wow, I cannot recall what it was about. Anyway, then we were dismissed. I left feeling defeated and miserable because I personally did not want to partake in the fast, nor did I want to come out to a corporate prayer. What is wrong with me?

## Am I Infected With Religion? Probably So.

I have come to realize that religion has even invaded my prayer life. Why is it that I cringe at times when I am asked to pray in public? Because religion and traditions have cemented a mindset within me that I have to use certain buzz words and phrases. That I have to make sure it lasts for at least 5 to 10 minutes to be effective, that I have some rest phrases to pause on like repeating "Father God" about 80 times. It has taught me that it sounds good to use scriptures based on His promises to make my point. I have been around some people who will begin to moan, clap, and say, "Yes Lord" and sing a few rambling runs of "Yes Lord" as a warm up before they pray. Some are so eloquent with their wording. "Most Gracious Heavenly Father of all the glorious universe..." I am not knocking your moaners and groaners. Hey, that is your way, but for me it looks like learned behavior. At most prayer gatherings, I would always feel defeated. I struggle with early morning phone prayers too. And again, I would beat myself up for missing the call or even worse, falling asleep on the call. Well, guess what? I threw the religious prayer file out too! I am now practicing being in constant commune with my Father. Keeping my mind stayed on HIM. I pray from my heart. It may be short and to the point or it may even be lengthy, but for sure, it is from my heart; it will be with expectation and it will also be filled with anticipation! Prayer is simply talking to the Father. It may even be the Lord's prayer. I love this prayer, especially the part about the Kingdom coming and for His Will to be done on earth as it is in Heaven!

## It Is NOT Going To Be Easy

A revelation came forth today. The fact is that I will always be a process. I will always have to maintain and contain. My very foundation was cemented in religious acts and as I increasingly became aware of this brutal religious spirit, I found myself becoming angry and very critical. The times I thought something was not right with me, thinking that I was not saved enough, not spiritual enough, not praying or fasting enough, now made me realize just how much time I've wasted trying to fix something that was invented to keep you always feeling like you need to do more to have God's approval. And so, I would repent and try to submit to authority more to the point that I took on the slave mentality. I did what was asked without questioning. My leadership was the word of God and the Bible was just a supplement. This system had me boxed-in and as I am discovering true freedom, I have begun to react like a jackhammer. Ripping and tearing down anything that looked, smelled or even acted religious. Relationships have become strained as I had come to a place where I now cringe just hearing religious talk. I am in the process of tearing down and rebuilding. The only problem was that when you "use a jackhammer", it creates a lot of noise, dust, and debris. In other words, it became "messy" and just like the heap that you see after someone uses a jackhammer on the cement, I looked back and saw a mess not knowing which area to begin clearing up first. I knew then that this was going to be a process for me. I had to lay down a new foundation and it was "love". Oh yes, I would continue to slough off religion, but my anger melted into love. Truly it became... "They know not what they do". Love began to fill my heart, and although the process is still painful at times, I know that I must maintain my freedom and keep my God-given Kingdom Authority contained within my mind. I must never let go of who I am in HIM.

# I REALLY Should Not Have Gone

I went to a conference. I did not want to go, but I went out of obligation and to be seen. No one tied my hands or put a gun to my head to make me go. No threats came forth. I went because I thought it would make me look less supportive and committed if I did not attend. My heart was not in it. Just being honest. The conference was at the beach. Let me type this sentence again. *The conference was at the beach.* It was beautiful and the weather was perfect. I wished I had come a day earlier since the facilitators only gave everyone a free afternoon to enjoy the oceanic views, excellent food, and great shopping. I arrived mid-afternoon with about three hours before the evening service was to begin. Once inside my hotel room, I immediately went to the balcony and took in my ocean-front view. It massaged all of my senses. The breeze, the smell, and the view were all extremely beautiful. I sat down for a few moments as I began to think about how awesome God is. He took such loving care and details to create such beautiful works. I began to worship Him right there.

The evening came around and after dinner I went to the event. As I came to the door, I felt so uneasy. I dreaded this and I was angry at myself for coming. Here I was again, attending, doing something that I truly did not want to do. I sucked it up and went on in. The church was not packed, but pretty full. The choir was singing wonderfully and I sat down in the back and tried to be opened-minded and glue a smile to my face. Again, no one made me come. I came on my own.

After the choir sang so beautifully, then came the first let down. A ten-minute offering sermon. I guess offering sermons are very popular these days since it can literally convict a twenty-dollar offering holder to squeeze out another ten dollars. Some of these sermons can make you afraid not to give. *Later for paying your mortgage. If you don't sow in this offering, a tree may fall on your home!* That may be extreme, but you get the point. Thousands of us who have been chained to the religious system have all been scared into giving or have given a fleece offering in hopes that God will come through because you have sacrificed so greatly. How great has that been for you? You cannot buy a blessing. I recall one incident that really got me extremely upset. A visiting Pastor told the congregants that God had revealed to him a secret for obtaining wealth. I mean this man was so dramatic and so full of enthusiasm as he shared his story that I believed him. Yep! For a few moments, I believed that God had indeed given this man THE KEYS to wealth and prosperity. My ears were at FULL attention while I waited for him to reveal the secret because at that time I was behind in many bills. I was so anxious and eager to hear, that had someone even cleared their throat, they would have gotten the evil eye! I wanted to hear every single word. I needed this information. Years of bad credit, poor judgements and not planning had really taken its toll on me and here was a man just a few feet away with a quick fix! Well, like I said, I eagerly awaited his revelation until the blow came. Yep, you guessed it. This man of God said that for everyone who would sow $1,000.00 in the offering, to meet him in room so and so…and he was going to give them the information! I am not kidding! My heart dropped and I was so angry. I just happened to be sitting beside one of the Elders of my church when this came across the pulpit and I turned and asked him this, "Since when did God's knowledge, which is given freely, become something that you sell for a thousand bucks?"

Mind you, all I heard were crickets from that point.

This conference was not cheap. The registration fee was $100.00 (Nice gift bags though). The hotel was a Hilton hotel, and the price was about $174.00 for a double bed. So, when the beautiful lady who was doing the offering sermon reminded those of their obligation to pay $100.00 in the offering went across the pulpit, I was shocked. Did I pay it? No, I did not pay the $100.00. I gave a small offering to the lady beside me and she went up to the plate. If these conferences are simply to raise money, then why not have a $100.00 plate dinner with some entertainment, words of exhortation and we can all go home? I would have preferred to have given someone $100.00 to keep their car or lights on to be honest.

After the choir sang another song, the speaker was formally introduced. A cute elderly ill lady came to the microphone and began to speak...And there I was again, in that familiar place where everyone around me seems to understand except me. She whooped and hollered to congregation's rants of "Amen...Yes... and repeat after me". Of course, I had to turn to my neighbor a few times. But look you all, I JUST DID NOT GET IT. Then she gave the recipe for living saved and holy. "Be loyal to your local church...Submit to leadership...Pay your tithes or you will be cursed.... Pray... fast.... dress holy, be loyal to your Bishop, be loyal to your First Lady...do not question your leaders... Submit.... And Submit again.... Be obedient to your leadership... Really, I could go on and on. But I will stop right here to say that this woman was so sincere in what she was saying. Her heart was filled with over sixty years of doctrines and traditions and what she said, she said it out of love, no doubt. But as I sat there, it made me feel sick to my stomach. And again came that haunting self-condemnation. Why oh why am I still going back and forth with this?!!! Can one lose their spiritual mind? My God, am I saved? Is something wrong with me? I prayed.

*Lord, I thought that Your message was so simple as well as powerful, but it is like You gave us a clear simple direction in your word, but we have added so much of our own man-made doctrines to it. After over 40 years, I still do not get what this stuff is. Lord, I so desire to be saved and go forth into what You have called me to do. Please, help me find TRUTH.*

One scripture that always puzzled me was: *Hebrews 13:17 (ESV): "Obey your leaders and submit to them, for they are keeping watch over your souls, as those who will have to give an account. Let them do this with joy and not with groaning, for that would be of no advantage to you."* Now, does this scripture mean that I am supposed to do all that my leader asks me to do? I looked up *submit* here in this passage. In the Old Testament, the word for *submit* is Kana, kabash and in the New Testament it is Doulagōgeō, Hypotagē, Hypotassō. The word for *obey* in this scripture is Peitho and the word for *leaders* is Hēgeomai for "your leaders" and Hypeikō for "submit". Peithō and Hypeikō does denote to submit. To dissect this further, let's examine this scripture in depth. In Hebrews 13:17, the text is not referring to leaders controlling you, governing you, or even in the sense of a wife being subjected to her husband. This passage is not to have leaders being like the Nicolaitans, which Jesus himself hated. It is not about being put under the leaders own personal authority! But rather those leaders who are Godly examples, who indeed keep watch over you and who are trustworthy. Who would not submit to someone whom they find trustworthy?

To confirm the context of the chapter Hebrews 13, verse 7 (ESV) says it all: *Remember your leaders, those who spoke to you the word of God. Consider the outcome of their way of life, and imitate their faith.*

Hebrews 13:7-8 (MSG) *Appreciate your pastoral leaders who gave you the Word of God. Take a good look at the way they live, and let their faithfulness instruct you, as well as their truthfulness. There should be a consistency that runs through us all. For Jesus doesn't change—yesterday, today, tomorrow, he's always totally himself.*

The best pastoral/ leadership example is Jesus Christ. The servant leader! How do you recognize sound leadership, build trust and guidance? By servanthood!

1 Corinthians 11:1 (ESV) *"Be imitators of me, as I am of Christ."* When leadership begins to put themselves first, that should be a red flag!

Let's look at 3 John verses 9 and 10 (ESV). *I have written something to the church, but Diotrephes, who likes to put himself first, does not acknowledge our authority. So if I come, I will bring up what he is doing, talking wicked nonsense against us. And not content with that, he refuses to welcome the brothers, and also stops those who want to and puts them out of the church.*

I believe that we should respect all. I do not mind submitting to someone that I trust, and trust is the foundation for all submission. Therefore, if I do not trust that you truly have my best interest for growing and becoming more Christ-like, but only have an interest in my finances and doing what you tell me to do, and making me feel manipulated or coerced into doing certain things, then I would have a problem with trusting you. I would have a problem submitting to a Pastor who would not even greet me in the hallway. Just walk pass you without saying a word.

The bottom line is this…make sure you know God for yourself and not just vicariously through your leaders. Begin to study and know His word for yourself.

The Bible says in Hebrews 13:7 *"Take a good look at the way they live, and let their faithfulness instruct you, as well as their truthfulness."*

A good contrite heart will be attracted to sincere leadership, as they will want to grow and have Godly examples. Am I willing to obey and submit? Yes, indeed. Am I willing to be manipulated and controlled? No!

## Laity, Laity, Laity...

I just happened to be on a social media site when I saw a
prominent First Lady making a statement about how Laity is
to act in regard to leadership. As you know already, I despise
separatism in the church. Therefore, I decided to look up the
word and find out how and why we use it so much within the
local church. For one, Laity comes from the word "Layman
or Layperson", which is a person who is not qualified in a
given profession and/or does not have specific knowledge of
a certain subject. In religious organizations, laity was derived
from Catholicism. It consists of all members who are not
members of the clergy, usually including any non-ordained
members of religious institutes, e.g. a nun or lay brother. The
word *lay* derives from the Anglo-French *lai* (from Late Latin
*laicus*, from the Greek λαϊκός, *laikos*, of the people, from
λαός, *laos*, the people at large)."

Although I do believe that it may have reached its peak,
(some may argue this point) there grew a huge gap between
the "laity" and the "clergy". Many people believe the higher
the ranks, the more untouchable you are. Some, due to the

downward spiral of morals in our country, even have armed security, four to ten men deep. Appointments must be made months in advance, with the Pastors having the option to consent or decline. Once, I witnessed people standing and bowing while having their hands postured in a praying position as a Bishop of certain denomination walked down the aisle. Yet, many of these individuals were talking and walking about during worship to who should have been the main attraction: Jesus Christ. As I said before, I was even once told by someone that I should never look a Bishop in the eye. Bowing your head; it is supposed to be a sign of humility and respect. Some old school beliefs would be to never say anything to a leader unless they speak to you. When I first heard this, I allowed fear to oppress me by never saying anything to any of the elite officials at all. Additionally, I refused to make eye contact...never wanting to sit near them or be close by them. I had a friend who had such a reverence for her Pastor, that she once told me of several occasions where she was in his presence and felt the fear of God on him, and always felt nervous and humblest before him.

In many denominations, there are rules for laity on how to serve the clergy. Here are exerts from one denomination: "Know the proper code of ethics and behavior toward the leader". Wow, you must know the proper code of moral principles and behaviors toward your leader. This may be a problem for some if you do not know the "code", especially if you were saved right from out of the hood or off the street and have not been indoctrinated into some institutionalized system. Next one, "Get to know your leader's likes and dislikes and govern your behavior accordingly". This must have been written in the 1950's or something. It kind of has the slave/master ring to it. So, I guess to be a good hand maiden or adjutant, you are required to study your leadership. OMGEEEEE!! I am having a flashback. I actually did that for one of my leaders. They kept getting short with me...even embarrassed me once. So, I decided to learn and observe all that I could, so that it would not happen again. I began to have it before they asked for it and I always made sure I was on post and ready. I knew what bothered them and I knew what made them happy. So, I guess you can say, I *did* know the code. At least "their" code. But can we stop right here and read Mark 10:44 (ESV)? "...and whoever would be first among you must be slave (Go: doulas or bond servant) of all".

I must tell you, I don't see many leaders who serve. Now, there are a few who I do see frying chicken and cleaning toilets. But for most part, the serving that I see is the laity serving the elites. And for some, I believe that delegation is considered serving.

Here is another rule: "Do not get involved with the leader's conversation(s) with the leader's colleagues. Step away and allow your leader the necessary privacy needed."

In other words, know your place. You can serve them, carry their Bibles, purse, slippers, briefcase, suits, lap cloths, adjutant kits, wash their cars, bring them juice and fix their plates, but keep your mouth shut. These elite colleagues are their colleagues, not yours. As if they belong to a certain section in the body of Christ and you don't. If you have been asked to drive them from the airport, recite your favorite scriptures or hum a song in your head. "Good evening or Good Day" is all you should say. If they talk to you, make your answers short and "safe". No compliments. This rule reminds me of when I was a young girl and my mom would tell me to keep out of grown folk's conversations. I guess for some saints, this rule may be needed. Folks can wear you out.

This next rule should come as no surprise. "Do not attempt to initiate conversations with your leader." What is amazing to me is that you are advised not to talk to your elite clergy; but yet, they are quick to receive a holy handshake! Wow! *(For those of you who are unchurched, a holy handshake is where a $100.00 bill or a grand check is slid in the hand discretely.)* Do not talk to me, but you can bless me financially at any time. Which brings me to this next rule. "Provide the necessary financial support as required in rendering tribute and honor to whom honor is due." I will not repeat myself. But I am tired of the pyramids. The "required" support for me to pay $150.00 towards someone who doesn't even return my phone calls, just so that they can pay their required $300.00 quota to someone who I cannot get within fifty feet of, by which they are required to give their $1,500.00 to some grand elite often times Bishop and it keeps going. I would rather pay someone's bill than to stand in a line for everyone to see me give towards something that I do not agree with at heart. Have I been guilty of doing this? Yes… shamefully yes. All because of a title, I have felt compelled to give so that I would not make my "church" look bad, as well as it was simply expected of me due to my "title". I recall once while sitting in a meeting, where an elite owed me rent money and yet came forth boldly to announce his $1,250.00 offering to the Bishop. I have since gotten over this. Forgiven. But you see my point here?

Here are other controlling rules: "You need to get permission from leadership to visit another church or attend another church function when your home-based church is having service." If your local church is depending on you to service in some capacity, I believe that it is only right to respectfully notify your leaders well in advance that you will not be there. If you are supposed to assist with the nursery or children's ministry, it could be problematic for you to be a no-show. But otherwise, to visit or show support to another ministry should not be decided upon by the elite.

Jesus made it clear that we are family! (Ephesians 3:14-15) And as within any family, we do have Elders. The church Elders are supposed to be those who are well established in the faith and are to be respected, not treated like an elite special society. God is the Head of the "family". It is this religious spirit that loves the hierarchy, which controls the laity. Didn't Jesus teach against that? Yet, we have it loaded up! Bishops, Archbishops, Superintendents, Elders, Great Apostles, Most Reverend, First Lady, etc. I don't care where you are; division will breed envy. All that a laity can offer is submission, while the elite mandates countless expectations and rules. Jesus made Himself so clear in Matthew 23:8-12 (NKJV): *But you, do not be called 'Rabbi'; for One is your Teacher, the Christ, and you are all brethren. Do not call anyone on earth your father, for One is your Father, He who is in heaven. And do not be called teachers, for One is your Teacher, the Christ. But he who is greatest among you shall be your servant. And whoever exalts himself will be abased, and he who humbles himself will be exalted.*

In the Book of Revelation in chapter two, Jesus makes some strong statements about something called, "the doctrine (deeds) of the Nicolaitans". This doctrine or belief included (among other things), the practice of dividing God's Church into a "class" system headed up by elitist leaders. Hello! Jesus said that He hated this type of system. Some denominations may claim to not practice such, yet they simply establish the same structure just using different wording. I have come to hate the word laity, and yet to hear the elites use it is so forthright.

I now feel apprehensive about having a "title" and a license.

## My Time Is Precious, Too!

Sigh.... Whenever any of my superiors, whether work-related or church-related asked me to perform a task or meet a deadline, I want you to know that I try to do it. I make notes on calendars and try to plan well in advance to prevent any confusion and frustrations just to complete the task. One thing that I do like about working at my company is that they let me know most things well in advance, even down to a change in schedule for meal hours. Thus, I too must alert them in advance to extended vacations. It works well for me and it works well for the company. I find last minute expectations come often within my arena, and it makes me angry to find that my time is not valuable to my leaders. I think that our church leaders should be just as respectful of our time as we are of theirs. Just saying.

## The Shade

One thing that I have noticed after being indoctrinated, as well as engulfed into the religious system is this: There are many social media haters. I hate to say it, but I have seen it; and unfortunately, I have even heard it. Everything seems to be subliminally laced with a spirit of competition these days. Un-Forgiveness is running viral amongst believers. They call each other's assemblies *cults*. Denominations throw shade on other denominations based on "their" belief systems. Pastors, after digesting their fried chicken and potato salad, casually ask the strategically poised question, "So, Joe...how many members you have now?" Only for Joe to reciprocate the question so that the initiator can expound on his congregation being "up to about a thousand now". Holy handshakes now create holy deals. But I guess if a Pastor was to give or bring you a $10k offering, you would tend to take him on as a "close friend and brother". And don't let members leave the flock to go to another local ministry. Wow!!! The former Pastor... the new Pastor ... as well as some of the members will stop speaking to them. Even unfriend them or worst, block them. How childish is that? It can make your head swirl. I admit that I once thought that I needed to be in the clique where everyone knew what was going on in the church. I mistakenly thought that people's business was for the elite to know, so that they could pray and cover them as well as the ministry. "Sister So and So" would go up for prayer and myself, as well as a small circle of ladies might go up behind her because we knew her "stuff". We knew that if the visiting Prophet hit it on the nail, she was going to holler and fall out, or that she was going to have a crying fit because she been holding "it" in so long. Because I knew who was having issues in the bedroom, at the bank or struggling with their identity, I felt a little big-headed. But for certain, I knew how to keep a secret and one thing a leader must do is learn to keep a secret...and I did. But. But...but...when you get around the people who also know the secret and begin to talk about it and give opinions and even laugh, that is another thing. The secret should stay in the secret circle. As I leave religion, I am left out of the "talk" now.

I am no longer in the clique and do not care to ever be a part of it again. What good did it do me to know personal information about certain "saints"? I mean I did pray, but I could have done that without the details.

## Questions...

When *he* got sick, so many things changed. When the diagnosis was grim, a morning prayer chain was formed. Everyone was urged to be online at 6:00 am to petition the Lord to heal *him*. There must have been close to one hundred people on that line at times. Folks from all over praying for healing. Praying for *him*. *He* being a man of God. The seldom seen Elders circles gathered around *him* and prayed. There were special services of prayer, and since *he* was so loved by many, just know that every single auxiliary had prayer for *him*, foremost before business. I loved *him*. I prayed for *him*. I made sure to rise at 6:00 am on a few occasions. (*Yes, that religious spirit made me feel like a chump when I overslept or just chose not to lead in prayer.*) The day *he* died I remember how I wept bitterly in my husband's arms. I had to leave work early. I could not function. I could not stop crying.

Others have died since, yet I have to wonder where were the prayer chains for them? Yes, their names were all on the sick and shut-in list, but where are the morning prayers for those who too, were given grim diagnosis or dealing with an illness? I thought we were forming a trend here. I thought that we would now have regular nights of healings. Who knows what might have occurred had we come expecting miracles, signs and wonders. I know that many thought that *he* was special, and in *his* own right *he* was. But, so are the other members. So many have died on that sick and shut-in list. We have so many programs. A program for just about every occasion. Where are the miracle services? Did they all go away when Brother Allen, Brother Lake and Sister Kathryn died? I HATE seeing people sick, especially the saints because I believe that Jesus died for our healing. We got it soooo twisted!!! We have programs to promote our platforms and show off our preaching skills with rhymes and rhythms, and people are sitting out there in the pews laden with sickness and disease. We master at raising an offering, but still cannot raise the dead.

How many times have you seen folks in a wheelchair at a service and the speaker doesn't even look their way?

Why? Because we love to practice the prophetic and not healing! We will run to a workshop on everything…. But, what about healing?

Jesus sho'nuff did a lot of healing y'all.

## Your Slip Is Hanging...

So...it started out as a sweet little gathering where He was always there. You called me sister and we loved one another as such. You referred to them as your brethren and the only echo you heard were laughter and prayers. And then, you became larger and the designated leader among you decided that it was time to find a building to accommodate the great and blessed growth that the Lord had given you. Growth must have structure, some rules, and guidelines are set up to make this "new found" institution run more smoothly. Teams are created and programs are set in place as more growth continues. Vision casting becomes necessary as the institution now begins to expand to accommodate the community through schools, daycares, and programs throughout. This institution called church continues to grow, and we find that where He was always present, we now have a protocol to usher HIM in. We have a "Call to Worship", and order of service with a timeline and a budget to meet. Soon the huge conglomerate which we pride ourselves upon and label it as a blessing, has become a consuming parasite that sucks the energy out of the members as they whole heartedly volunteer, sow their tithes and offerings, give their time and run to make each and every mandated service. Sundays have become...exhausting. The leader is constantly monitoring the costs of what is coming out and what is going in. Program after program, session after session. You find yourself working to keep the church going...working to keep the reputation sturdy as it sucks you dry. Oh, you look cute. Godly. But down by your ankles, I see a dingy white laced edge dangling.

# Getting Out Of My Comfort Zone

Religion thrives upon approval and comfort; and like many others, I like comfort. Sometimes we will do what is most comfortable, even at the expense of changing for the better! We will sit, or better yet, remain positioned because we like it, because we are used to it, and because it makes our flesh feel great. Thus, because we remain in this cemented status, religion brings her flattering approvals. She recognizes two types of people: 1) The ones who are faithful to her and help her enlarge her territory. By which she will reward with titles, status and praise "giving honor to whom honor is due". 2) Those who are a threat to her ploys, whereby she will manipulate, play the victim or even defame to get these threats to her kingdom eliminated.

As I am continuing this detox, I can truly feel the discomfort. For years I remained and served, and I must admit, many times I did it for recognition from my leader. I wanted him to know how much I loved him, how I was committed to the vision of the house, and that I was willing to submit under his authority with full surrender. My faithfulness was my way of thanking him for helping me grow spiritually and for his continual watching over my soul. This was my perception. I believe, based on my commitment, I did receive recognition from time to time. And yes, it felt good.

But I can tell there is a change. As I seek the Kingdom of God, I couldn't care less about recognition from my leader or anyone for that matter. I am so paranoid of being sucked into a religious realm. When you begin to seek after TRUTH, seek after the one true GOD and HIS Kingdom, nothing else will matter to you. I don't care about the accolades; as a matter of fact, they make me nervous because I cannot perform according to the script.

## Protocols

The protocols of religion are exhausting and will have you feeling like you are a substandard being. Religion has always reminded me that I have a proper code to follow, and that I must behave a special way.

I always looked awkward or out of place. I am sure some people have their comfort zone in all of these religious protocols. For me, the opposite was true.


## Widows

You can tell a lot about a church by how they care for their widows...

## I Fell Back Into The Rut

I have done it to myself again. I should have said no, but
I did not. I am tired and I miss seeing my children.
Family time is very important to me. Now, I feel like I
am in some type of tormenting tug of war because I really
do not want to participate; but I gave my word and I do
not have the courage to say no. Why don't I want to
participate? Well, because it is another religious toxic
program, completely predictable, and structured down to
the "Turn to ya neighbor and say…And high-five three
people and say…" My God…what is happening to me?
This is what I have been taught all my life. It is supposed
to be predictable because we need order. Opening prayer,
the praise team or choir will come with two fast songs
and two slow songs. Announcements will be made,
acknowledgements will be made, and the ushers will walk
certain dignitaries to their reserved seating up front. Sigh.
Then comes those offering sermons. Now, 30 to 45
minutes of persuasion mingled with scriptures twisted to
make one feel that they are either required or obligated to
give in the offering. On top of that, you have the one

hundred-dollar line, two-hundred dollars, five-hundred dollars and one-thousand dollars please-come-forth lines. Now, comes the introduction of the speaker…after the choir sings one selection, the next voice you will hear will be Bishop "Lollipop". Please stand out of respect for the God in him.

The choir will sing one song and Bishop "Lollipop" will acknowledge the 10 to 20 Pastors and the "Angels of the house" …etc. He has to now set the atmosphere. So, he will say a few religious phrases with some rhythm and rhyme to the crowd. The organ will begin to ramp up a bit setting a tempo, waiting for just one emotionally excited sister to begin dancing in the spirit. At that point, the musicians all tap-in as others "catch the spirit" and thus, you have a shouting marathon. I find it humorous as well as interesting how Bishop "Lollipop" will tell the audience, "Y'all sit down, sit down… quiet on down…" and as the audience begins to settle down some, "Lollipop" will let out a catawhaller of a scream and again. Next, we have a "Spirit Breakout", with people running, shouting and bucking. This is now the second leg of the marathon with a few sideline heaps going on as well. Fifteen or twenty minutes may go by with more familiar religious phrases thrown in like kindling to a fire. And finally, "Lollipop" will wipe his forehead with his hanky as the marathon ends and everyone is now bent over doing spiritual cool downs. "Lollipop" lets us know about the great time he had in Detroit where Bishop "Bubblegum" is presiding. You will hear about how God moved...He will tell you that Mother "Lollipop" sends her love, and then he may share a testimony or a funny story. And after about 40 minutes, he will tell you to turn to the book of _____ chapter _ verse __. "If you have it, say amen." He will read the scripture and give the title, and sometimes even a subtitle. If the title has a popular ring to it, you will hear the audience agree and applaud with anticipation. Bishop "Lollipop" will then preach. Now, if he is an older gentleman, he can't whoop and holler but for so long, because all of that activity along with sweating will make him tired. He may even get a cramp. *(And all this time, we thought he was making that face because he was quickening in the spirit.)* The response of the crowd tends to determine his volume. A younger fellow can go on much longer, and he may even jump over chairs and still have enough energy to pray for folks. At the end, you will hear the organ begin to play the "cool down" medley. If you have a house full of saints, he may just go straight to the "seal your blessing" offering, especially if there were praise-breaks in the middle and end of the sermon. Now, I know we already took up an offering. Remember, we were asked to give our best offering three hours earlier. This offering will normally be based upon the theme, the scripture, or some symbolic numeric phrase. This too will be categorized…the one-hundred dollars, fifty dollars and twenty dollars and finally, the "bring what you can because you don't want to miss out on this blessing" offering.

Afterwards, Bishop "Lollipop" will be escorted out by his entourage. This is determined by the size of his ministry. It can range from just a couple or up to five or six brothers. The neophytes will be carrying his Bible, briefcase, and suit jacket. There, "Lollipop" will be given his due honorarium and either led to a private meal cooked just for the dignitaries or driven to a special restaurant. The laity will be informed about the fish dinners for sale and reminded to come back on tomorrow. The house Pastor will say the benediction and finally we can go home. Right now, I feel ashamed of myself and I hate the mental place where I am right now.

# I May Be Wrong...

My perception may be off...BUT as I have now had the
liberty to travel and visit other churches and denominations as
well as fellowship with various saints, I've noticed
three types of groups within the church...

Group A: <u>they are always on time</u>. When there is a
conference, they pay on time... sometimes ahead of
time. They appear to be well dressed, but conservative and
very sincere about their walk with God, although they can be
cliquish. To play there, you got to pay! They follow
leadership and love the arts and music. They shout on
occasion. They give from their heart...never being forced or
compelled, they get whatever is needed. They love titles
because they believe it promotes order. They will create a
title to keep the order. The five-fold teachings I found are
expected to be carried-out within the leadership. The
congregation sits and listen. They get encouraged to do better,
get emotionally charged. Then, they go home.

Group B: <u>they are always late and when there is an event or conference, they pay at the last minute</u>. Their style ranges from the pricey Saint John suits, to the worn and torn. They are very sincere about their walk with God. They follow leadership almost exclusively and love to shout, sing, and fall out. They give from the heart and they give out of obedience. But they also give out of fear. They believe in "sealing your blessing". They too love titles. To them it promotes order as well as establishes a hierarchy that honors their leaders. Their titles are displayed and to not be downplayed at all. They are to be respected and you are reminded to *pay honor to whom honor is due*. However, the five-fold system seems to be split. It is the Pastor who is the Teacher, Evangelist, Apostle all in one…and then the "House Prophet", who is however subject to the four-fold Pastor is allowed to only project what the Father has given him when allowed by the four-fold Pastor.

Group C: <u>they too are always on time…many will come early.</u> When there is a conference, they will pay on time or early. They will raise money to help others be able to come. Their style is neat and conservative, but not too pricey. They are sincere about their walk with God, but they are always seeking more of HIM. They walk with leadership. Sometimes they follow, sometimes they lead. They experience joy accompanied by signs, miracles, and wonders. They give deep and will give amongst each other within, as well as throughout. Money seems to come from nowhere to accommodate their needs. Amazingly with this group, you will find the authentic titles, but they seldom have them on display. The five-fold are all within the body. Some are Apostles, Teachers, Evangelist, Prophets and Pastors.

As I detox from the religious system, I am now becoming more drawn to those of Group C. Each group has a dominant mindset. When you have a mix of Group A and B, you got a problem. With these two mindsets within the same pool, division comes for obvious reasons. The elite B's will not tolerate being ignored of "their" gift. They will seek to expand inwardly. Conferences, conventions, and galas...while the A's will argue to expand outwardly. Expressing the need to get "their" name out in the community. Eventually, what happens is that the A's will wander off until they find an "A" group and the B's will add a wing and continue to ensure that they have an awesome praise team. Group C only thinks globally, which is too far beyond A and B's vision. For A and B, their mission funds are about as close as they will get to thinking globally. A and B have street maps, while Group C has the world map.

Just my observations...I may be wrong. Either way...This struggle, this detox...as I eliminate, I realize that what I thought was part of my spiritual ecosystem is what has been clogging me up. Yet, with all of MY personal revelation and perceptions, I am still having a hard time with this.

## Church Meetings

I get butterflies whenever we have a mandatory church meeting. I have been to ones where I left feeling bruised because I was not "doing enough". I've also been to some where major decisions were made by the board and I had to sit and pretend that I was excited and in agreement with everything that was said. And then, there were some where I just wanted to walk out and leave. Pastors, let me tell you a big secret...if your congregation trusts you, then they will WILLFULLY submit to you. As long as it is not controlling. You don't have to bring in anybody or tell the people to submit fifteen hundred times a year!!! People may fail to submit when:

- They never see you serving. The mark of a good leader is to serve and be willing to serve.
- Inconsistency. When leaders say one thing and do another.
- Members do not have clarity of the vision. I have had some leaders who never feel like they owe anyone an explanation for changes or acquiring funds.

- They do not trust you. It is almost impossible to fully submit to someone whom you do not trust.
- They feel used.

In the *church*, God has appointed Elders or Pastors (shepherds) to oversee the flock (Acts 20:28; 1 Pet. 5:1-4). They are not to lord it over the church, but rather to be examples to the flock (1 Pet. 5:3; 2 Cor. 1:24). On every level, those in authority are never in absolute authority. Every leader will give an account to God!

The text is clear that the church should submit to *godly* church leaders. Abusive leaders should be confronted and removed from office (1 Tim. 5:19-21).

## Longing For Miracles

For those of you who have seen bonafide miracles…The dead
being raised, instant healings and occurrences like gems
appearing from Heaven, and just supernatural unexplainable
Godly encounters, let me say this with all love and respect:
I…(if possible) envy you in a holy way. I yearn to witness
my Father's amazing works to the point where I am floored
with great Godly fear and trembling. He has healed and
continues to heal. He does so many great things, but to me,
they can be considered behind the scenes so to speak. I want
to see the blind eyes open…I want to see the dead raised…I
want to see a limb grow back. That's right, I said grow
back! I want to see tumors pop out! Lord, I so want to
witness this. Why in all my 42 years of being in church have
I not ever seen a bonafide miracle? Why have I NEVER seen
a funeral interrupted? Sometimes I wonder, am I the cause?
Did I lack faith?

I remember when I was about 12 years old, and this lady in
my little country church had a stroke and the Pastor called her
up to the altar to pray for her. Let me tell you that my

excitement and anticipation was so thick you could cut it. I got so excited you all...and why not be excited, I was about to see a miracle! And due to the fact that my eyesight was terrible to the point where I had to wear coke bottle like glasses, this meant more to me than you could ever imagine. Cause I knew that if God healed this blind lady...He was certainly going to heal me of my bat like 20/100 vision! My eyes were glued on the Pastor as he took out the oil and poured it into his hands. Let me stop right here. This again caused a stir within me, because he did not seem to be doing anything random here...he had all his "tools" handy. The Bible, oil, and his huge giant hands. He laid his hands over her eyes and with a loud voice, my Pastor prayed for sight to come back into this lady's eyes in Jesus' name. And when he asked her to open up her eyes and let him know if she could see him...well hey, that was it for me. I was ready, well we all were because that church was so quiet you could hear a feather drop. But when she shook her head and said no, I was so disappointed. He went on to pray for about five minutes and finally he gave her the bottle of oil and told her to anoint her eyes every day. The blind lady was not just led back to her seat, but she was led out of the door. Was it her? Was it the Pastor? Was it the congregation? Was it what I have been told thousands of times…that, "It just was not God's will"? Hey, I know God is Sovereign, but I also believe HIS words. "I will give you back your health and heal your wounds, says the LORD." In Jeremiah 30:17, He says that He is the God that Healeth thee!

Again 42 years in the institutionalized church system and I have NEVER seen blind eyes opened. I have never seen limbs healed. I am sad to say that I have heard too many testimonies of Cancer being "healed", only for it to later-on come back with a vengeance and take the person home to be with the Lord. BUT yet, I believe and that is why I am burning to be a witness as well as be used as a vessel for signs, miracles, and wonders. I am now beginning to believe that the religious church has not seen many miracles because we have grieved the Holy Spirit with our time constraints, protocols, and tainted doctrines. By HIS grace and those who have hungered and believed HE has graced us with miracles on occasion. But when was the last time your church had a healing service directed totally by the Holy Ghost? When was the last time you recall the Pastor asking the blind man to come up front for prayer or the lady in the wheelchair? We are all about two fast songs and two slow songs, the Pastor preaches you happy and leaves right afterward to go do the same thing at his two other services as members still exit sick, broke, depressed, and demonized.

There is something key that Jesus said that may be our answer. Matthew 10:7-8 (KJV), "And as ye go, preach, saying, 'The Kingdom of Heaven is at hand.' Heal the sick, cleanse the lepers, raise the dead, cast out devils: freely ye have received, freely give." Wow! Look here...We must proclaim that the Kingdom of God is at hand! Well, in order for us to proclaim that the Kingdom of God is at hand, then we must know the Kingdom of God, we must be a part of the that Kingdom and know how to operate in that Kingdom. It is like someone coming along and saying, "Hey, I got what you need right here...I am loaded with the goods." Look at this verse: "Jesus called his twelve disciples to him and gave them authority to drive out impure spirits and to heal every disease and sickness." (Matthew 10:1, NIV) So they were given authority to do so. Did not we gain that authority when we became born again? Did not we acquire rights to this authority as joint heirs with Christ? If indeed we are of the Kingdom of God, then as ambassadors, do we not come with all that the King has to offer?"

Kingdom is the key here…not just a buzz word either. But it is comprehending the fact that the Kingdom of God is God's wealth, rights, reign, and rulership to restore and reclaim all that was lost in the Garden of Eden. It is we who are to bring the Kingdom and it is we who are to restore the Kingdom. And as ambassadors, the King has bestowed upon us all that is needed for us to fulfill our God given assignment.

Do you want to see miracles happen on a daily basis and not just on YouTube? Meaning that you want to do the King's work for the Kingdom? Slough off your religious mindsets and begin to "Seek ye first the Kingdom of God". I may be off, but I believe that healing is for everyone. I am reminded of Matthew 12:15 (KJV), "But when Jesus knew it, He withdrew from thence: and great multitudes followed Him, and He healed them all;" He healed them all. Why can't we?

## Onion, Green Pepper, and Celery

I am sad today. I want to scream! But all I can do is cry. Is this it? Another program? As many programs and conferences that I see popping up, you would think that we would have the fire of God upon us so heavy that no sick could walk beside us, nor would a sinner ever feel at ease. But here we go again. It is like a food trinity up in here. Onion, Celery, and Green Pepper on program. Yeah, the Onion, who will pull tears as she ministers from her emotions. She's crying and has us out in the audience crying. She will have you promising to do better, asking us to repeat after her, "It's not ova till HE says it's ova". Next up is Green Pepper, who will scream, hoot and holler; and have you turning to your neighbor, turning around three times, high fiving until the palms of your hands feel like they are about to explode and of course, she will make you get that confirmation shout in. And for our last course, there is the Green Machine itself! Celery; you can eat the seeds, the stalk and the leaves. Celery is the deal closer. Oh, you know the celery; they are experts at raising an offering. You will hear about the seed, first fruits, or a special one-time offering of sowing to seal your blessing.

I am so tired of programs! I do understand that for some churches, programs are the only way they can pay bills. But wouldn't it be great to have a program just for people who need to pay a bill? Have some individuals submit three bills within certain limits with a guarantee that one of the bills will be paid off. I think that the Father would be pleased at that.

## Do Not Touch Me!

I was screaming in my head. "Do not...I repeat...Do not lay your hands on me. You are operating under the spirit of Jezebel and anyone with a grain of discernment can see it!" Everywhere I look around, I see their eunuchs. Some of them are even friends of mine, but I am not going to allow them to touch me. For a minute, I panicked. I did not want to cause a scene. I dodged the line acting fake and scurried off to my seat. I don't care how expensive your suit is or what your title is. Do not touch me. I don't need to deal with any more religious spirits.

## The Great Platform: The Must-Have for Spring

The great platform...I hear this a lot from aspiring leaders within the body, as well as seasoned leaders. I was told that the goal is to get your name out there by attending as many speaking engagements as you can because you never know who may invite you to speak at the one great event, which may land you a national platform. Wow! Sounds like a dance competition where everyone wants to make it to nationals? So, you study, and I guess...practice??? And you begin to get real good at presenting and learning what the judges like...*oops, I mean the congregation and pulpit crew.* Three points and an atomic bomb-like closing. When you think you have mastered it well enough, you can then do a Facebook live run. Everyone's dream is for it to go viral...right? I mean that is the goal to have that national platform. You can finally share that "DEEP" *sure to make'em shout* message you been holding onto. This platform can set you up real nice, so that when you write your books and sell your CDs it can bring in a great profit. Look, that is what I see and hear from some leaders, y'all. I have heard this! I have been asked to pray for so and so, because they were speaking for a few minutes at a

Convocation or special event and that this might bring them a national platform! I am not really astute on the church business side, but I think that if God wants to bless you with a national platform, then it will happen. Your gifts will make room for you. *Proverbs 18:16(KJV) A man's gift maketh room for him, and bringeth him before great men.* Just preach Kingdom and follow HIM. If what you are doing requires a National Platform, then HE will get you there. Let's face it: some would not even be able to handle it. It might even cause dire consequences if you rush it. Is it not HIS agenda as well as His Platform? I bet those who rightly have national platforms directed by the Holy Spirit have had some mind-blowing struggles that have come with it. Some suffered greatly for the sake of HIS CALL, and yet we want to treat it like a Status Symbol and Holy stamp of approval. You have no clue the cost of the OIL. All you see is the shine.

Got to be honest...My desire would be for a national awakening of the Kingdom and I would LOVE to be a part of the great movement. But until HE sets it up, I will stay put. The invite might sound intriguing and my flesh may want to say YES! But unless He says go...you can call me Kizzie.

## Foot Pain With An Attitude

Wow…I was asked to stand and remain standing. I listened to what my obligations were…I listened to additional announcements that were initially left out. I listened to a funny story that was told and I gave a fake laugh. A trail of leaders walked in and me, along with everyone else, clapped for them as they remained stoned-faced and sat down. My feet were now beginning to hurt and I truly wanted to take my seat. At first it was just a burning feeling and I tried to ignore it; but as the seconds passed, that pain became real! I could have slapped myself for wearing the strappy shoes where you have to unbuckle them to take them off. And I knew these were my one-hour shoes to boot, but I had no idea that we would be standing this long. I kept standing as my feet were having a sword fight in my shoes, until I finally saw a light coming! Finally, the old testament scripture has been read. I said "Amen" with the crowd and was about to take my seat on the second row and guess what? "Oh…no you didn't ask us to remain standing." My Lord…this lady now is addressing the leaders!! Don't she know that according to church protocol, you do not have to officially address the leadership when you are saying a scripture??!! The house has already been addressed! I am getting a serious attitude right now, as the pain meter lets me know that I am closing-in on 30 minutes. She begins with addressing the Bishop on down to the laity and friends. By now, my feet feel as if they have turned against me. Somehow, I find a way to slide those shoes over my thick ankles and the shoes come off! As the New Testament scripture is being read, I now ask the question that probably every three-year-old has asked and has gotten pinched for. "Why are we still standing, and those people up there are sitting down?" I plop right on down on my seat and dare someone to look at me contrary. I question myself on the ride home. Did I really have to get all extra about standing? Next time, wear jeans and sneakers, and sit in the back.

# Teacher

I love good teaching. As a matter of fact, I know that my gift to the body of Christ is teaching. I also love to be taught as much as I love teaching! Especially when it is done in a practical way, using relevant examples that are easily relatable as well as applicable. I remember one time listening to a gentleman minister who was to my knowledge fluent in Hebrew and Greek; I guess you would call him a Bible scholar. He used a lot of big words. He told us that he was going to give us an exegesis of his text…Why not just say I am going to give you a critical explanation of my text? Now I know what this meant, but to Mother Eighty-nine or Sister Twenty-two, this might just go over their heads a bit. This "Scholar" continued on with so much of his impressive rhetoric that within ten minutes, I was done. Zoned-out. My mind went to what I wanted to eat after church.

As a teacher, you need to know your "class" or sect. Jesus was an excellent example of a teacher. There are 18 verses in the Bible that reference to Jesus being the master Teacher. It is one of the five-fold ministerial needs for the body. Yet, amazingly we know of Apostle So and So, Prophet So and So, Evangelist So and So, Pastor So and So...But, who do you know who is Rabbi or Teacher today in our Christian denominations? I have seen some elaborate ordination ceremonies with layers of clothing, tassels, and rings. I have seen Pastors installed and Apostles installed. I have seen Evangelists titled and received, as well as the noted Prophets of the House and Region. But I have NEVER seen a Teacher get ordained as a Teacher. Why is that? Are we trying to elude to suggest that the office of a TEACHER is not as important to the body as the Apostle or Prophet? I guess the Pastor and Teacher are one. I know some may have dual roles and y'all, there are some who will eat the whole pie and tell you they fully operate as the Apostle, Prophet, Pastor, Evangelist, and Teacher. (Which I personally do not believe.) Hummm...gonna study this.

# The Silence Of The Sheep

The Silence of the Sheep amazes me. What do you do when you know what you are in or doing is unbiblical? What do you do? When the visiting speaker claims that in order for you to receive your blessing, you must seal your blessing with a $101.00 seed? When you see the money pyramid being built right before your eyes; and yet, you still get in the line? When you really want to visit or fellowship with another church and your Overseer says that you cannot? When you are told that if you leave, you will be cursed or if you question your leader, you will be labeled as out of order and God, the Father will not be pleased with you? When you are told to dress modestly, which means to lessen the intensity and you see First Ladies bling out like comets? When you find yourself desperate and you begin to tell a leader of your concerns, and all they can say is "I know"? When you see the elitism and nicolation character emitted throughout with special seating and accolades, while the widows, sickly, poor and homeless go unnoticed? Silence when you see leaders who cannot hear the cries of the hungry because of the noise from building their own platforms and brands? You know that what he said was wrong, but you turn your head the other way, simply because he is a leader?!! You do not question leadership? Is that in the Bible? Spiritual Coverings…Spiritual Fathering… The House Prophets, The Archbishops, the different pools of anointings and mantles. This seems to be the new spiritual fad. Yet, I do not see any biblical grounds for it. Can I wear pants? Can I wear make-up? Can I dye my hair? A few years ago, it was sinful. Did God change HIS mind?

I know that you are not perfect, and neither am I. Yet, you would sit me down in the 60-Day corner just because I question you or disagree with you…

I am amazed at how some KNOW that they are embedded into a religious system of twisted doctrines, but remain silent due to friendships, prestige, status, connections, money, and platforms. When all you know is the sun by which you revolve around, you are bound to keep going in circles.

## Smiling As I Write This

How do you know that you are beginning to embrace the Kingdom and becoming free of the religious system? When your primary focus becomes about seeking the Kingdom of God. I say this to say, that in the world that we live in I have found other "kingdoms" established and functioning. You see, everything has a nucleus. The world claims a "King of Pop", a "King of Soul", why there are even kings of food chains, hotels, king crabs, the silver screen, etc. It is our nature to proclaim *something* as the two best; the top and the ultimate king. We do this because innately, we are always searching for the ultimate euphoric ruler or system. Voltaire said that "if God did not exist, it would be necessary to invent him". Therefore, as I look at myself, I can now see where I once worshipped other "kings" in my world to a place where I am consumed with seeking the Kingdom of God. Worldly matters are irrelevant, the gossip has taken on a deaf ear, the present situations have been placed on the back burner as I focus or learn more about HIS Kingdom. Matthew 6:33 (KJV) and Jesus told us to, "Seek ye first the Kingdom of God and His righteousness." In verse 10, we were instructed to pray that the Kingdom come. This is some potent kool-aid I am drinking! Because the more I truly seek, the more I can honestly see a change within my total being. I understand Paul! "He [God, the Father] has delivered us from the domain of darkness and transferred us to the kingdom of his beloved Son" (Colossians 1:13, ESV). The Kingdom becomes your world as well as within you. For indeed, *the kingdom of God is in your midst* (Luke 17:20-21).

It is just as if I have been given a promotion as an Ambassador of the King. My service is for the King and I must do his bidding. I am now beginning to speak differently, think differently, and see differently. Every day I await orders to find out what the assignment is. Sometimes it is on the job training, somedays I have to dig deep in the Bible (manual) to gain a clear understanding. Sometimes it is just listening. As you grow into seeking the Kingdom of God, you will develop a Godly consciousness in which there is never hardly a minute where you are not aware of HIM. This is where relationship begins to become knotted! This is the place where you begin to learn of His tempo, so to speak. This can be a lonely place. And if you get every prayer answered, then great for you! But I am finding that it is also a place of building trust and faith, as well as preparation. We do not become Kingdom citizens to sit around. He is preparing us for HIS service. I must add that the religious spirit makes me angry as well as sad these days. I no longer criticize or argue the point with those who are within that religious system. I was bound to a religious system that had me thinking I was losing my mind. I was confused but dared not to question. I did not feel it but pretended to. I did not understand it but repeated it. I would do it even when I did not want to do it, and I saw things and turned the other way. No more. I think I am on the right road. Very narrow and long. I am sure to stumble a bit. But I am not getting off this road.

## Bullseye On Your Back

There are thousands of people out there who do not know HIM. They know of HIM. This religious spirit is ugly! (Matthew 23) Is this not what our religious system does? It puts us in a box and burdens us with rules to keep and practices set up to engage God. I actually grew up thinking that there were certain things that had to be done in order to get God's attention. I thought that the prayer had to be a certain length and it had to be emotional. I thought that the dress, the prayer shawls, the oil, the Bibles, the head coverings, the moans and groans were essentials to getting HIS attention. This was like a mindset for me. I thought that those with the layered robes were closer to God and could get my prayers answered. I thought that the elite titled leaders always had to have special seating up front and at the table, and that I would be out of order to not do what they told me to do. I thought that I had to have a spiritual father, a spiritual covering, a church covering, a denominational covering, and a head covering. I thought that I had to submit even if I did not agree or want to, or I could be cursed. I thought sharing my opinion was an example of being out of order. I never really got in the game. Therefore, I've always felt like an odd ball. A certain keyed-up ramp of the organ never made me jump, and for that reason, for years I thought that something was wrong with me. It is taxing enough to examine your heart and soul each day within, let alone to examine your heart and soul within the external expectations of the church. Keeping track and finding excuses for the Sundays missed, communions missed, meeting missed, workshops missed, conferences missed, prayer meetings missed, state meetings missed. So, then indeed for some, church is their life. Whereas I want no parts of it.

Kingdom living will produce a bull's-eye on your back. There is going to be a price. People will not understand you. They will think that you are out of order, rebellious, uncovered...you name it. Friends will begin to subliminally unfriend you. Initially, it will be a lonely place as you begin to grasp the Kingdom concept, which is the rule, reign, and government of the King.

## We Both Pee and Bleed

Should there really a difference between the elite and laity? I guess my question would be, if yes, then WHY? Let me try to rationalize this in some way. Can it be for physical reasons? Well, let me see. We both fell at the same time. When Adam sinned, WE sinned. We both are saved now. We both have DNA, we both pee and bleed, we are of the same Kingdom, Phylum, Class, Order, Family, Genus and Species. We are both made of dirt. Thus, I would think that we are both the same, so that cannot be it. Could it be an economical reason? Money? I just cannot believe that because one wears Saint John's or Chanel and I wear "Whatever is on sale" makes us so different. After all, if I really wanted to wear designer suits, I could surely find them toward the end of the year at the thrift stores. Better yet, I can get one at the consignment stores or even rent one these days. A mere suit with a tag cannot place you above me. Dollars? I don't think so. Even if your anniversary purse was sixty grand, that would not do it. I have the same amount, except that it is just dished out over twelve months. We both work, am I correct? I just happen to either own my business or work a mainstream job, while you work for the ministry. But we both work...don't we? Naw...we still the same, and guess what? If I invest my money wisely, I can end up with more than that. Plus, we both still got to pay Uncle Sam, so with all of that being said, I just don't think that economics really supports you being a level above me. Is it spiritual then? Well, spiritually the Father sees us both as HIS children and I have been told to work out my own salvation, meaning that you will not be able to get me into Heaven. When I stand before Him, I will be alone. Let me see, spiritual gifts have been imparted into me by the same Holy Ghost that was sent to both you and me. There is one spirit, one God, and one baptism all given to all who believe. I really do not believe that anyone can determine who is the greatest or least here based on spirituality. So right now, it appears that we ARE on the same level, which I must say is looking good for a unified body right now. So, what about titles? Do you think that this could indicate that you and I are not on the same level? Wow...is the Teacher which is part of the five-fold less valuable than the Apostle? (Incidentally, I believe an Apostle ranks higher than a Bishop.) No, of course not. All are equally important toward the functioning of the body of Christ...oh and your church as well. Do not get me wrong...I respect the title, I respect the office, I even respect you due to your age as well as your "seat". I would give you the honor as due for the position that you hold, same as I would my supervisor, president or commanding officer. But that does not, from any biblical point, mean that I am beneath you. What knocks this off the shelf is that today as a meager lady of laity you would say that I am not on your level, but if by chance tomorrow I married a Bishop or became an Arch Bishop's wife, you then view me as being on the same level as you are, just by title alone. So, that means with my locks or curls I am not on your level, but with a title and a tall blinged-out hat I am not on the same level as you? Come on...stop! Let's all get on HIS level together. Whether you lead or I follow, as long as we are doing the work of the Kingdom, it does not matter. Instead of training others to be handmaiden to serve your needs, let's both be handmaidens for HIM.

# The Religious Resume

Why do some of us post our spiritual itinerary listing of all

our speaking engagements? I guess a practical answer would

be so that our friends or associates, if nearby, can come and

support us. It must be a blessing to be speaking to a crowd of

unknowns, only to see some familiar faces smiling back at

you. You could say "Green Peas will make you sneeze" and

still get an amen or two. On the other hand, it should not be

considered a measurement of your spiritual success. As a

leader in the body, it should never come across that your

anointing is crowned by how many speaking engagements

come forth, as well as how big your platform is growing. I

have seen posts where someone may say, "Just got a call to

come to Africa! God is doing it!" I believe that God will

open the doors to do Kingdom work, but we must be careful

that certain engagements are a direct sign that you are in the

will of God. How many prominent Pastors and speakers of

the gospel have had secret sins embedded within their life all

hidden by their charismatic voice, talent and platform? It may

just be me, but at times it seems like a contest on social

media or a way of sending subliminal messages to let

everyone see your week-long itinerary filled with engagements. Oh, and don't even let someone get invited out of state. Honestly, I once felt the pull to use the measuring gauge of occasions as a tool of indication of God's approval, as well as man's trust or opinion in my calling. That does not even sound right, does it? But we are in a time where this is becoming the mainstream, the national gage so to speak. An addendum has been added to the book of "How to have a National Ministry and Major Platform". And then...I see that there are certain venues that if you by chance get invited to speak, your spiritual career can propel into greater opportunities. How many would love a chance to speak at certain mega churches in Florida, Georgia, Texas, and California or to become one of the spiritual sons or daughters of Pastor Big Name? There is such a thin line of demarcation as to this concept being indeed God ordained or Man ordained. We must truly discern each offer and by all means make sure that it is aligned with HIS Kingdom purpose. For some of us, the bridle will be painful because we simply love what we do. We love ministering, we love sharing the gospel of Jesus and when invitations come forth, sometimes the flesh grabs it and runs with it, leaving our spirits weak. I know the offer came from Cali and the theme is exactly the scripture that you have been studying for a whole month now, but beware! It might not be His agenda. It takes a mature Kingdom centered person to judge this. Indeed, HE said "go". And by all means, we should go forth and proclaim that the Kingdom of God is at hand. However, make sure you go prepared and full. Prepare, get on the line, get primed and positioned to hear the sound of the gun. And when you hear it, take off running. This will always gain you a victory.

## Sniff, Sniff...But I'm Good!

When I realize the damage that religion has done to me and the years that I have wasted, my eyes get filled with tears. Yet, looking at the grace and mercy that HE bestowed upon my ignorance and still allowed me to see and experience HIS mighty works, again I get teary...knowing that HE loves me without and within.

## You Won't Understand Unless You've Been FREED

The religious spirit…it is one of the most destructive spirits I've ever had to deal with. I was genuinely saved along with being filled with the Holy Spirit and immediately, swooped up into the religious habit. And that is what it does. You become indoctrinated in learning what you must do to be saved, act saved, and stay saved. You pray for at least one hour, you must read your Bible daily and you must attend church services to get fed. You must pay in every offering, you must show your face, your support and your allegiance. You must attend classes, workshops, and conferences. You must take the spiritual gifts tests and answer the call on your life. You must submit and follow leadership. You must dress a certain way and carry yourself a certain way. Your home church's service must have priority over other services. You only have an opinion if you have authority. You do not look a Bishop or high-ranking church official in the eye, you must raise your finger up when leaving your seat. You must not question leadership, Elders or any elite authority within the body of Christ. To seal your blessing, you must give in this offering as an act of faith. You must trust God with the first fruit offering, the sacrificial offering, the seed offering and such. Oh, the tears I cried over me breaking every single one of the rules above. Feeling like a failure in constant...I mean constant repentance mode. God, will I ever be good enough for You? When I finally got the revelation of the answer, relief came. "No", religion had me doing religious "twists and turns" and constantly in a mindset of what can I do to make God happier. What can I do to insure my salvation and be a living witness? After all, I did not want to let God down. This spirit had me feeling low when I was not doing what it required of me and yet, it had me all pumped up with pride when I did happen to pray for two hours, attend every service and sow a one-hundred dollar offering. I was still jacked-up and always feeling like I was under a microscope, questioning my salvation, repenting almost hourly, looking for judgement and curses to come and trying to look good in front of leadership. No one put a gun to my head to allow this to happen, but I allowed this religious spirit to seduce me into almost losing my mind. I kept telling myself that it has to be "better than this". And it was! Jesus said, "Seek ye first the Kingdom of God..."

## Open Letter Written For Those Who Wish They Could Say It

I'll have you to know that I have been delivered and I have been set free and I do not share my testimonials to try and poison anyone against "church". I understand that it can come across as being critical, rebellious or asserting toward sowing discord; therefore, I am careful about what comes out of my mouth. However, when asked, I do share the truth. When asked my opinion, I do share it. But maybe that is part of the problem. I only share when asked. Maybe this "truth" needs to be expressed, regardless of whether asked or welcomed. I must ponder that. Now, I understand that there are a few of my spiritual siblings who asked, because they feel that I am a "safe" ear for them to express their concerns about the "family". But I also have a few siblings whose only objective is to try and bait me. That does not work, because I love my church family. I love them right where they are and for who they are. They are wonderful people and I am grateful for many foundational truths that I have learned from the institutional church.

My problem is that they are trying to hinder me from becoming and growing more into what God wants me to be. To put it simple: Mom and Dad...I've grown up!

A toddler needs to be taught how to properly eat, dress, and behave. They must be trained on how to use the potty, how to sit still, hold the bottle and such. My church taught me in excellence on how to not stumble during my first steps. They gave me my first milk right from the bottle, and I loved every ounce of it. I was a healthy baby. I drank all of my milk. These bottles nourished me as a babe until eventually, I learned how to feed myself. One pea at a time I would eat until I mastered the spoon, fork and eventually knife. As I mastered these things, my Elders admonished each and every achievement. As I grew, they gave me responsibilities. This groomed me into learning to follow as well as lead. I grew up steadily and well nourished. I was primed with proper manners. I learned how to use my inside child sounding voice. They taught me how to study, how to manage and gave me great examples of a Godly life. As a matter of fact, my church did such a great job at training me, that it encouraged me to dig deeper and to seek the Father all the more. I grew and grew until finally, I grew up! And now being able to stand on my own two feet and share my growth to others, you want me to remain seated on the pew and eat your pureed meat from only your spoon? You helped to ignite this passion to touch others, yet you want to keep me in the *prayer pen* with you? *Reciting from the prayer reader...*? You allow me to walk outside; but yet, you have me tied to your hand to keep me near. You want me to dress a certain way, not talk when you are talking and be the good little obedient adult which you helped raise! Listen...I love you! I am proud to be your offspring. I look like you...I talk like you...everyone says that they can tell that I am yours. As a child, I grew to react to your voice. I did all that you asked and to be honest, I was fearful of disappointing you or being sat down in the 60-Day corner. I respected you. I supported you. I got your glasses, ya water, ya shoes, umbrella, coat, pocketbook, Bible, checkbook, mints, handkerchief, notes, hat...

I gassed your car, washed your car, and made sure no one messed with your car. I kept a lookout for you when you drove up and made sure you and your family had a seat. I cut your grass, I cleaned your home, and I baked your favorite pound cake. I gave whatever amount was asked for. Budgeted for your anniversaries, appreciations, birthdays, first fruits, One Day's Pay, One Month's Pay and even participated in those predictable offerings that correlated to the Chapter and Verse of guest speakers. I wiped the lint off your suit and shined your shoes without you ever knowing about it. It made my heart jump with joy to give you holy handshakes! I kept my ears open for you, blocked the door to the whiners and my siblings who loved to wear you out with their drama. I would be the bad guy. I protected you. I backed up far away when "grown" folks talked to you, never repeating the gossip I heard. I even stood and watched you eat that fried chicken when I was starving. And now, hearing the call of my Father to leave and go out and do what He has called me to do, all you can say is that I am out of order?!! Are you serious? Did you not teach me, train me, and encourage me to learn how to hear from God on my own? You said seek HIS face. Well, I did! And He told me to go out and make disciples, to tell of the good news, to lay hands on the sick and spread the news about the Kingdom of God! I cannot do that in the highchair with a titled bib around my neck. I am tired of the pacifier. It does not taste good anymore. I want meat. I served you well…and that was done out of love. I loved you and I thought that I was serving God as I served you.

Beautiful One, I am not bound, at least not anymore. I actually think that *you* are the one who may be bound. You appear to act entitled. Often reminding the "laity" of their accountability to you. You seem bent on teaching the proper twisted doctrines of religious protocols and how to act in the presence of a leader. My institution taught me to serve well. Wherever I go, it is apparent that I was "raised" well. You did a good job, but now it is time to let me go.

I want you to understand that I know why you are such a hindrance. It is rooted out of love! This is the only way they know how to keep me near. By holding on and controlling. You were done the same way and to you this is the right way. It is your way of holiness.

Run, Beautiful One. Get out of this vicious cycle of programs, conferences and meetings all geared to keep the fat institutionalized conglomerate alive and running. What does it offer you in return? It drains the "laity", it keeps you up at night worrying about how to continue to cover the TRUTH and maintain status…and wealth. Sigh…

But I so understand…I too was once blinded by the gauze of religion. You call what I have done a "disconnect", but I call it a great escape.

## Really Yawl??

Wait a minute...wait a minute...Please stop! Stop saying that I need a spiritual covering. I did my research. It is not even biblical. It came out of a movement from four well-known Pastors at the time in the 1970s, by which it became part of doctrines and parlayed into all types of religious hype, birthing sons, daughters, and spiritual Dads with a vine of control. You say I need a spiritual covering??!!! No, I don't! Where do you find that in the Bible?!!! This again is an example of twisted doctrines used to manipulate the body of Christ by leaders. The only covering I need is Christ. And by the way, the four Pastors who started this "covering lie", renounced it later on. This religious spirit tried to seduce me into almost losing my mind. I kept telling myself that it has to be "better than this". And it was! Jesus said, "Seek ye first the Kingdom of God" ...

## My Priority

May I remind you my dear leaders...You are NOT my priority. It is about HIS vision. I must align to HIS vision as a priority. Seek ye first the Kingdom of God...THIS is my priority. This is what HE called/commanded all of me to do. The hierarchical belief that claims only an anointed few can hear from God is a lie. I encourage everyone to know God for yourself. The FATHER wants a relationship with us. Not one only filtered through a leader. We have some robotic Christians who act as if the preached word is the word of God and Bible is just a supplement. Twisted. Know HIM for yourselves. When I stand before God..."they" won't be there with me.

## Tears

I truly despise the religious system and what it has done to the body of Christ. I feel deep with the pit of my soul a mourning; a grief stirring. Could this be the Holy Spirit grieved at what is being done in the body? That the Lord has allowed me to experience how hurt HE feels at how we have put His words in a shredder and glue them together to fit our distorted doctrines? Oh God, Your grace and mercy are truly great. Your love is amazing, for only such can be that You, still out of Your kindness, allow the body of Christ to proceed in some twisted ways. I have detoxed from the religious system to where, when I see, hear, or sense it, I begin to feel angry and sad. Yet again, I find myself in a lonely place. Doubts come only by seeing how the religious are the mainstream. What if what they are doing is right and I am truly out of order or wrong for the most part? Only the truth will set me free.

## My Passport

At hand, there is a Kingdom and I am a citizen of this
Kingdom. My citizenship has changed; thus, I must now
begin to focus on the culture, order, and rules of my new
government. I am becoming more familiar with the King's
dialect. This Kingdom is upside down! Everything that I
thought I was normal is abnormal here. For example, you
give to receive, you love those who hate you and in order to
live, you must die! Everything is centered on words like:
Restoration, Reconciliation, Redeem, Re, Re, Re…I left
everything behind to become a citizen of
this great Kingdom. Those who did not come with me, I
left. Basically, I came naked, but I am not worried. The
King has garments for me. Designer originals; couture, just
for me. Garments of praise and garments of righteousness are
hanging in my closets. I have armor as needed and swords
marked with truth and a shield of faith. All that I have need
of has been provided because in my country, we are a
commonwealth, which means the King provides
everything. No welfare, just HIS care. As a citizen of this
Kingdom, I have been granted the title of Ambassador.

This means that I carry my Kingdom within me. Where I go, the Kingdom goes, where I stand, the Kingdom stands. That also means that wherever I stand, I carry HIS full backing, power, and company! A new country, a new job with great benefits to boot! With ambassadorship comes assignments, which is always on-the-job training. We meet daily and He gives me instructions on what is needed to provide expansion of HIS Kingdom. I go where HE sends me, and I do whatever HE asks me to do. I am a servant of the King, and I have a GOOD Father. My mindset is changing and my focus is beginning to become like a laser. Nothing else matters, but HIM. The King loves, the King lives, the King longs for all to become reconciled back to the homeland, the Kingdom of God.

When I stepped through the door so to speak, my spirit jumped within me as if it knew exactly where I was. My flesh was overwhelmed with emotions of love and peace, but oh, my spirit zoomed-in as if it had been waiting for this moment all of my life. I am where I need to be now, aligned with other citizens/brothers/sisters/ambassadors/comrades and warriors who are in the Kingdom of God to simply do HIS work. As I have learned, battles still will come and pain just don't go away; the wounded sometimes die, and even citizens have absconded due to call. But it is a decision that is grounded in trust and a heart that yields to complete surrender. You got to see the flag of glory waving...the big picture so to speak. It is from victory to victory, but you may get scars, but like a medic, HIS spirit is always with you. Compared to eternity, the battles are nothing.

## Packing My Bags

There is a lot of religion in me. Not as much as I used to have, but I still have a lot. Tent revivals, prayer bands, prayer groups, basement churches, store front churches, churches without bathrooms, country churches, city churches, big churches, small groups, gatherings, prayer circles, prayer lines, 5:30 AM prayers, midnight prayer, district meetings, union meetings, revivals, convocations, impartation lines, this conference, that conference…it has been a way of life for me. Had I simply stayed in the religious lane and not wandered into the realness of the Kingdom, I would have still made Heaven my home. I would have continued trying my best to be at every service, being obedient and submissive to my Pastor, Deacons, Elders, and Ministers. I would have attended every conference and made sure to give my time and money to the house of God. I would have served as much as I could and taken every class offered on insuring my spiritual growth. I would have continued offering my gifts and talents to the body of Christ, as well as making sure to spend ample time with the intercessory prayer group and serve as my rightful duty to an auxiliary. And…at the ripe of age of let's say 90, I would simply die and go to Heaven. I think of Acts 1:8 (KJV) *"But ye shall receive power, after that the Holy Ghost is come upon you: and ye shall be witnesses unto me both in Jerusalem, and in all Judea, and in Samaria, and unto the uttermost part of the earth."* I would have probably stayed right in Jerusalem, and if appointed to a state position, I might have ended up in Judea and Samaria. But honey...I've been in Jerusalem for 40 years! On to Samaria!

## Not Long

You won't stay wrong long if you really want to do right. As I suspected, all hell is breaking out. I don't care. I know who I am; A Kingdom Ambassador. I can now add three things that the enemy should have never allowed to happen as far as I am concerned:

1. Salvation
2. Deliverance
3. Knowing who I am = FREEDOM

## Religion and Kingdom

Religion is all about what you do and "KINGDOM" is certainly about who you are. Who are we? What God requires of us will take HIM in our lives to accomplish it. Religion sucked the life out of me. It had me flipping my lips with my finger and always trying to do something to get HIM to love me. As I continue to embark on a new journey of learning more and more about the kingdom of God, I have a new-found freedom. I am discovering who I am in HIM. No fluff. Those religious pulls are not as strong as they used to be. Seems like the closer I get to HIM, a lot of the things I thought were so monumental seem small now. Will I go back to church? Well, I am the church you know. But I do hope to find a remnant of people whom I can do family with. I will be looking.

## Feeling Lighter

I'm feeling lighter. Not sure if it is because I've cried a pound of tears or because I have finally let go of many religious ties. It was a painful separation, but I knew it had to be done. I now sit by the brook. Right now, there is a brook of water and HE sends my daily bread every day. For now, I will rest until the brook dries up. Growth is here. Preparation is here. Once I leave from here, I will be changed.

CPSIA information can be obtained
at www.ICGtesting.com
Printed in the USA
BVHW081636090321
602112BV00007B/459

9 781734 254068